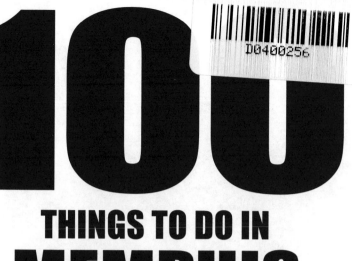

100

THINGS TO DO IN
MEMPHIS
BEFORE YOU
DIE

Crosstown area, page 35.
Photo credit: Samantha Crespo.

100
THINGS TO DO IN
MEMPHIS
BEFORE YOU
DIE

• •

SAMANTHA CRESPO

REEDY PRESS

Library of Congress Control Number: 2016931467

ISBN: 9781681060408

Design by Jill Halpin

Cover photo: Overton Park Bike Arch, page 68.
Photo credit: Jamie Harmon, courtesy of the artist, Tylur French.

Printed in the United States of America
16 17 18 19 20   5 4 3 2 1

Please note that websites, phone numbers, addresses, and company names are subject to change or cancellation. We did our best to relay the most accurate information available, but due to circumstances beyond our control, please do not hold us liable for misinformation. When exploring new destinations, please do your homework before you go.

DEDICATION

To Pepo and Nina (again), and to Memphis.

• •

CONTENTS

• •

The Arts (and Artful Souvenirs)

• •

• •

Food and Drink

• •

Music and Nightlife

• •

Additional Tours and Resources

PREFACE

When Edition 1 of this book debuted in May 2014, it was a good time to be in Memphis, Tennessee.

Fast-forward to 2016, and it's only gotten better.

Today, experiences that I could merely preview in Edition 1—music halls of fame, expanded bike paths, and anticipated restaurants, to name a few—are alive with people. The neighborhoods we embraced then have deepened their hold on us, encouraging start-ups, community gardens, public art, and stirrings in additional districts. The fuel? People making a commitment to Memphis, or, as we say locally, choosing 901.

This explains why Edition 2 is more than a routine update of my first 100 things. Those updates are here, but you'll find them punctuated by fresh ideas: some to celebrate the changes in our surging city, some to spread the love to other Memphis musts.

As a reminder, this book works for several audiences:

1. To the travelers worldwide who come, or dream of coming, to Memphis in search of its spell: Welcome. I'm always warmed by the torch you carry for this city. Use this book to plan the Memphis pilgrimage you've dreamed of, and then some.

2. To Memphians in need of rekindling their love affair with the city, or of experiencing it in new or unexpected ways: Let's play a game I like to call "Hometown Tourist." The objective is to quash excuses. I understand them: You moved to the 'burbs and downtown isn't right around the corner anymore. You've been there/done that, and anyway, you don't have an out-of-towner on your arm. You've always wanted to do

• •

(insert wish here) but (insert excuse here). Let this book be your motivator to get out and do those things: some old, some new, some you've always wanted to do.

3. To current and expat Memphians who, unaided, see the beauty: Curl up with my love letter to our city.

How to use this book:

- Because newbies as well as natives turn to this book, expect a mix of obvious and less obvious experiences. You'll be briefed on the biggies (usually from a new or insightful angle), but you'll also be primed to scratch the surface.

- Always call ahead to establishments. Though addresses, phone numbers, websites, dates, and hours were accurate immediately prior to publication, things change.

- As you read, you'll notice I've organized suggestions for you by theme. I've also grouped some of the entries by neighborhood, and into seasonal suggestions, beginning on page 136.

And, as many suggestions as I've included over these hundred-plus pages, I've left at least as many out. Follow my discoveries, and tell me about yours, at samanthacrespo.com.

—Samantha Crespo

• •

4E   72

ELMWOOD CEMETERY

Elmwood Cemetery was established on August 28, 1852. Buried here are Memphis pioneer families; 14 Confederate generals; victims of the Yellow Fever epidemic of 1878; Governors Isham G. Harris and James C. Jones; U.S. Senators Kenneth D. McKellar, Thomas B. Turley, and Stephen Adams, who succeeded Jefferson Davis in the Senate; E. H. Crump, prominent political leader for decades, along with 21 other mayors of Memphis; and Robert Church, the South's first black millionaire.

TENNESSEE HISTORICAL COMMISSION

Elmwood Cemetery, page 19.
Photo credit: Samantha Crespo.

HISTORY AND HERITAGE

Dear reader, this section isn't even trying to be alphabetized. Rather, I'm presenting it loosely by geography to help you plan your exploration. We'll stay in downtown Memphis from pages 4 to 17, then move to other parts of the city and just beyond.

National Civil Rights Museum, page 14.

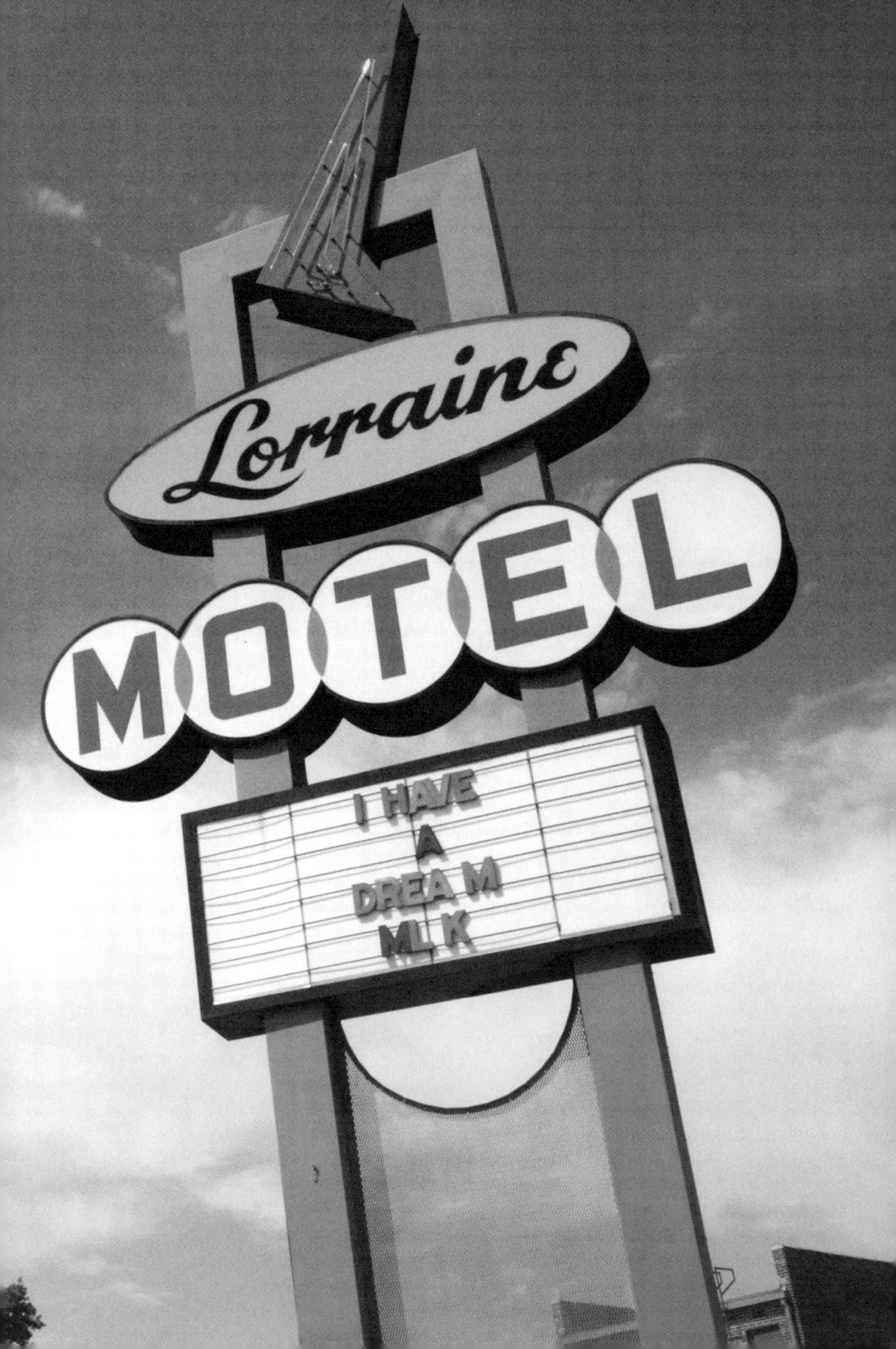

DO BEALE STREET
BY DAY

Beale Street Historic District

Sure, neon lights by night are mesmerizing. But there's a quietude to Beale Street by day that's something else. Start at the Elvis statue, on Beale between South Main Street and South 2nd Street, and continue east where the Brass Note Walk of Fame memorializes music-makers from preacher/songwriters to jug bands to Justin Timberlake. Scan for historic markers (here's to you, Ida B. Wells) and don't stop 'til you've reached W.C. Handy's house, relocated from Memphis's Soulsville neighborhood, where the 25-minute guided tour is all you'll need to see where Handy lived sometime between 1905 and 1918. Today, it's trimmed with family and career photos and the air of knowing that the street and city just outside inspired classic compositions.

To dive deeper, check out the audio walking tour of Beale Street from the Memphis Rock 'n' Soul Museum, page 114. This is Beale like Beale can't even show you: Numbered stops on a souvenir map conjure a time when orchestras filled these clubs, blues acts filled the streets, and Handy found inspiration inside Pee Wee's Saloon. Keep the headset for the day, pausing for lunch or anything else. For me, that's fresh-squeezed lemonade from A. Schwab, Beale Street's oldest business/time capsule.

A. Schwab
163 Beale St.,
901-523-9782,
a-schwab.com

Memphis Rock 'n' Soul Museum
191 Beale St., #100,
901-205-2533,
memphisrocknsoul.org

W.C. Handy Memphis Home and Museum
352 Beale St.,
901-527-3427,
wchandymemphis.org
Closed Sunday and Monday

HAIL THE
AMERICAN QUEEN

American Queen Steamboat Company

The *American Queen* cruised her inaugural season in 2012 from her homeport in Memphis. She's designed to capture the romance of the river with throwback décor, an onboard "riverlorian," and genteel, multiday itineraries along the Mississippi. You might not have the vacation days or dollars to cruise with her, but you probably have an hour to tip your hat to her while she's docked. March through December, Mondays, 4–5 p.m. is prime time: Stop by Beale Street Landing, page 10, watch as passengers come and go from their land excursions, and listen as the paddle wheeler's six-piece "house" band plays Dixieland jazz. Check the cruise schedule before you go to confirm docking location and dates.

251 Riverside Dr., 901-654-2600,
americanqueensteamboatcompany.com

RIDE
THE RIVER

Memphis Riverboats

Memphis Riverboats's *Island Queen* sternwheeler isn't mechanically faithful to her 19th-century prototypes, but she looks the part. Anyway, you'll soon be glued to the Mississippi River panoramas from her open upper decks. March through November, buy tickets and board from Beale Street Landing, page 10; sightseeing cruises run four miles down the Tennessee side of the river and back up the Arkansas side for a 90-minute roundtrip. Chances are, James Gilmer will be your captain, tour guide, and chief mingler. His script covers Tom Lee to towboats, but don't leave without meeting him personally: It's Gilmer's stories of running the river during the 2011 floods and of being among the first African American riverboat captains that are truly epic.

251 Riverside Dr., 901-527-5694,
memphisriverboats.net

COVER 954 MILES
IN FIVE BLOCKS

Mud Island River Park

The address below leads to a paid parking lot where you can board a monorail for an island in the middle of the Mississippi River. The island holds Mud Island River Park, where the Mud Island River Museum introduces you to native tribes, steamboat-era characters, and Delta musicians forever swept in the river's flow via artifacts and replica vessels like the *Belle of the Bluffs,* a recreated paddle steamer you can board. The roundtrip monorail ride costs $4, or you can buy a package that adds access to the museum. But wading through the island's Riverwalk, a geography lesson disguised as a splash park, is free, and my family's favorite island to-do. Let the little ones slosh about as you linger over the stories of each city detailed by this scale replica (30": 1 mile) that condenses the 954-mile flow of the Lower Mississippi River into five blocks. When you reach the Gulf of Mexico, represented by a million-gallon pool, rent a pedal boat or savor for free the wide-open view of downtown Memphis.

125 N. Front St., 901-576-7241,
mudisland.com
Open April through October, Tuesday–Sunday

GET SCHOOLED
BY THE SHELBY COUNTY HISTORIAN

Jimmy Ogle Tours

Jimmy Ogle knows so much Memphis history, you practically have to run on his walking tours to keep up with him and his train of thought. The Shelby County historian gives at least 50 free tours annually, including Tuesday tours of downtown streets and riverfront parks, walks through Memphis's historic Fairgrounds, and my personal favorites:

About five times a year (select spring and fall Sundays at 2 p.m.), Ogle explores rarely charted territory: the sidewalk along the Memphis & Arkansas Bridge, the only legal sidewalk across the Mississippi River within 500 miles. He begins in Crump Park with a 20-minute orientation to the river and its bluffs, bridges, and barges before making the march. Go at your own pace and as far as you like along the one-mile stretch suspended 100 feet above the river.

Third or fourth Thursdays monthly at noon, meet Ogle outside the Judge D'Army Bailey Courthouse downtown. Exterior statuary, an antique courtroom, relics from an 1835 bust of Andrew Jackson to a historic cuspidor . . . there's a story behind everything you'll see on this tour, and Ogle tells it like no one else can.

jimmyogle.com

BONUS:
5 MORE WAYS TO RELISH THE RIVER

1. Get RiverFit. Page 65

2. Paddle a scenic tributary. Page 62

3. Return at night. During Twilight Tuesdays in June and July, Beale Street Landing's grassy roof becomes a starry-skied movie theater. Bring a blanket and the family around dusk to catch the screenings. August through October, Tuesday nights are for Dancing on the Dock: informal salsa lessons set to a DJ's beats. Both event series are free. *251 Riverside Dr., memphisriverfront.com/venue/beale-street-landing*

4. Sit while the kids splash. As I see it, the best playgrounds work for kids *and* parents. Beale Street Landing earns my approval with a colorful splash pad my daughter can shriek through while I sit, surrounded by the downtown Memphis skyline and Mississippi River. *251 Riverside Dr., memphisriverfront.com/venue/beale-street-landing*

5. Take it from the top. Memphis's new Bass Pro Shops at the Pyramid is many things—bowling alley, indoor swamp, hotel, and one of the largest single-retailer locations in the world, among them—but I like to rise above all that. Let the elevator zip you up 28 stories, step out onto a glass observation deck, and gaze into Arkansas, over the Mississippi River and downtown Memphis, to the eastern edge of the city. *1 Bass Pro Drive, 901-291-8200, basspro.com/pyramid*

QUIZ YOUR CREW
AT THE COTTON MUSEUM

Cotton Museum

I frequently direct families to the Cotton Museum, and here's why: You start on the floor of the Memphis Cotton Exchange, active in this building from 1922 to the early 1980s. The room is decked as it appeared in 1939, with oral histories, artifacts, and exhibits added. Next, you cross to the Exploration Hall, a collection of vibrant, interactive exhibits: Guess how many pairs of jeans one bale of cotton yields; drench denim with "rain" to see what engineered fiber can do; learn about the dreaded boll weevil in a light-up display; examine a replica gene gun; pick up a cotton sack. Feeling proficient? Challenge your crew to the Hall's cotton trivia game: Spin the wheel on the wall, answer questions, and move a tractor marker to keep score.

65 Union Ave., 901-531-7826,
memphiscottonmuseum.org

STICK AROUND
AFTER THE DUCK MARCH

The Peabody Memphis history tours

Daily at 11 a.m. and 5 p.m., five North American mallards waddle down a red carpet and splash into, or out of, the lobby fountain of The Peabody Memphis, very much like they have since 1933. In the morning, arrive early and stay late: Crowds begin gathering by 10:30 a.m., so the earlier you show, the better your chance of scoring a table, a photo with the Duckmaster, and a Bloody Mary. Kids, don't be shy about sitting right on the edge of the red carpet, or asking the Duckmaster for a keepsake lapel pin. Following the procession, march yourself to the concierge desk to reserve a spot on the 11:30 a.m. history tour ($5 for hotel guests; $10 for the public). The Duckmaster himself leads this hour-long junket, spilling with stories of Tommy Dorsey and his orchestra playing the Skyway Ballroom; Vernon Presley and son signing Elvis's first RCA contract, on view in the hotel's Memorabilia Room; and "secret" architectural details (the lobby's faux skylight abounds with them).

149 Union Ave., 901-529-4000,
peabodymemphis.com

GET
ON BOARD

Memphis Railroad & Trolley Museum

Imagine an age when 50 railroad arrivals and departures chugged in and out of Memphis daily. Hard to visualize? Not at the Memphis Railroad & Trolley Museum. Located inside circa-1914 Central Station, the museum displays original timetables along with scale replicas, model train setups, a Thomas & Friends–themed nook for young enthusiasts, and technology: manual and electronic switches, even rail signals you can push a button to flash. If you like aged spaces as much as I do, ask a staff member to point you to the station's bygone waiting room, now a special events venue where an antique call-board hangs and sunlight streams. Then, ask for a look inside the former baggage and freight tunnel, strewn with century-old baggage carts.

545 S. Main St., #121, 901-590-3099,
mrtm.org
Closed Monday–Thursday

REFLECT ON
THE NATIONAL CIVIL RIGHTS MUSEUM

National Civil Rights Museum

The National Civil Rights Museum unveiled a $28 million overhaul just as Edition 1 of this book was published. Today when I tour the museum, I don't feel as though I'm merely passing by exhibits. Rather, I feel pulled in by them: Across a floor map, I can trace channels of the Atlantic slave trade in my own footsteps; in a scaled-down church, I can hear songs of protest. At listening stations, I can select oral histories from people who lived during Jim Crow and tracks recorded during the Black Arts Movement of the 1960s and '70s. There are even listening posts outside of the museum now, broadcasting personal stories related to Memphis's 1968 sanitation strike, the Lorraine Motel, and Martin Luther King Jr.'s assassination. For me, the view of the room where he spent his last night remains the museum's most powerful point.

450 Mulberry St., 901-521-9699,
civilrightsmuseum.org
Closed Tuesday

MAP MLK
IN MEMPHIS

MLK-connected sites and African American heritage tour operators
If you've toured the National Civil Rights Museum, you've stood where Martin Luther King Jr.'s time ended in Memphis. Trace his steps back on a driving tour. Mason Temple (930 Mason St.), today the international sanctuary and headquarters of the Church of God in Christ, gave the pulpit to King and his "Mountaintop" speech on the eve of his assassination. Next, navigate to the East Memphis corner of Colonial Road and Sea Isle Road, where a historic marker remembers sanitation workers Echol Cole and Robert Walker, killed nearby on the job in February 1968. Their deaths sparked the Sanitation Workers' Strike that brought King to Memphis; a new mural on South Main Street between Huling and Talbot Avenues amplifies the strike's rallying cry, "I am a man," in bold colors. Round out your MLK itinerary with lunch or dinner at The Four Way, page 82, and a visit to the Withers Collection Museum & Gallery, page 50.

Want to go with a guide? The group bus tours listed below will take you to MLK-connected sites and other African American heritage points around Memphis, from Slave Haven Underground Railroad Museum to LeMoyne-Owen College. Heritage Tours will even take you on a road trip to the Alex Haley Museum in Henning, Tennessee.

A Tour of Possibility, 901-326-3736,
atopmemphis.com

Heritage Tours, 280 Hernando St., 901-527-3427,
heritagetoursofmemphis.com

DON'T TAKE THESE HOMES
FOR GRANTED

Magevney, Mallory-Neely, and Woodruff-Fontaine historic homes
You might not realize the momentousness of touring Memphis's Magevney and Mallory-Neely homes. They escaped the overworked wrecking ball of urban renewal only to be shuttered for years by budget cuts. Today, their doors are open again, so show 'em you prize 'em by visiting. For its part, the 1830s Magevney House is Memphis's oldest residence, diminutive with similarly intimate displays like the family Bible and Mrs. Magevney's wee garden out back. Tours are complimentary.

In contrast, the circa-1852 Mallory-Neely House is a study in opulence, a 25-room Italianate villa flaunting 95 percent of its original décor. Your eyes may need a rest taking in the first-floor double parlor, which includes Antonio Canova's *Psyche Revived by Cupid's Kiss*, a Louvre holding, replicated in solid marble over onyx and supported by a brick pillar in the basement.

Next door, tour the Woodruff-Fontaine. Built as a three-story French-Victorian in 1871, the manse today stretches six stories tall thanks to the addition of a tower. Tower access was granted to the public in fall 2015, so get on up that ladder: At the top, imagine the scene when the street below was nicknamed Millionaire's Row, with a view clear to the Mississippi River and a collection of 30 grand homes. Elsewhere in Woodruff-Fontaine, eye for gems from Elliott Fontaine's journal to a room stuffed with vintage fashions.

Magevney House
198 Adams Ave.,
901-523-1484,
memphismuseums.org/magevney-overview
Open first Saturdays monthly

Mallory-Neely House
652 Adams Ave.,
901-523-1484,
memphismuseums.org/mallory_neely-overview
Closed Sunday–Thursday

Woodruff-Fontaine House
680 Adams Ave.,
901-526-1469,
fontainehouse.org
Closed Monday and Tuesday

MAKE YOURSELF AT HOME
IN CENTRAL GARDENS

Central Gardens Association Home & Garden Tour

You're driving west along Central Avenue when the houses hulk. Your vision goes all front porches and porte-cochères and arbors. You want to slow down, study the homes, peek behind their parapets. Do it Sunday afternoon following Labor Day during the Central Gardens Association Home & Garden Tour, celebrating its 40th year in 2016. This National Historic District and Level 3 arboretum is truly a mix of homes grand and petite, old and new-made-to-look-old . . . a popped-up encyclopedia of early 20th-century architectural styles. A changing lineup of six to seven private residences annually ensures you'll see a variety on the tour, and docents at each home will ensure you know your Queen Annes from your Craftsmen, then coax out family heirlooms. You might even catch an antique car show along the tour route.

While you're in the neighborhood, stop by Grace-St. Luke's Episcopal Church, where a turn-of-the-20th-century depiction of the ascension, designed by Louis Comfort Tiffany, awes over the chapel entrance.

Central Gardens Association Home & Garden Tour,
901-343-6242,
centralgardens.org

Grace-St. Luke's Episcopal Church,
1720 Peabody Ave., 901-272-7425,
gracestlukes.org

REPEAT:
ELMWOOD CEMETERY IS A PARK.

Elmwood Cemetery

True, Elmwood is a cemetery. But it was established in 1852 as a park, with bandstands and a trolley delivering citizens to its gate. "They came to visit their ancestors, but also to socialize in the fresh air," reminds Kimberly McCollum, Elmwood's executive director. (If you were waiting for one, consider that your invitation.) With a little planning, get in on year-round events from lunchtime lectures to October's Twilight Tour guided by costumed interpreters. Personally, I take my Elmwood hushed: Park along any curb—roads wind throughout the park—and set out with your camera and/or running shoes and/or dog and/or nothing at all; you've got 80 acres and 160-plus years of history, as told by fairytale trees and romantic statuary, to cover. For an instant itinerary, loop the cemetery's mile-long perimeter or call on the cottage at the entrance for the $10 audio tour or $3 tree map (Elmwood is a Level 2 arboretum).

824 S. Dudley St., 901-774-3212,
elmwoodcemetery.org
Cottage closed Sunday

SHRINE ON

Crystal Shrine Grotto at Memorial Park Cemetery

Scene: 1930s Memphis. E.C. Hinds visualizes a different kind of cemetery for the city: one where nature, and art inspired by it, prevail over high-rise grave markers. Enter Mexican artist Dionicio Rodriguez and his peculiar talent for sculpting and coloring concrete. Access Memorial Park Cemetery today from Poplar Avenue and you'll come to Rodriguez's Fountain of Youth and Wishing Chair first, modest preludes to his Crystal Shrine Grotto. For a preview, imagine a geode swallowed you: Sparkly stalactites and wall formations surround. Biblical vignettes set within present statuary backed by mosaics and metallic murals. Outside the Grotto, trace garden paths and sculpted foot bridges, rest on a carved bench to watch fish swim in the Pool of Hebron, peer into the castle-y Cave of Machpelah, and stand inside Abraham's Oak, an immersive example of Rodriguez's faux-bois technique. One more thing: You can find Isaac Hayes's grave directly across from the Pool of Hebron.

5668 Poplar Ave.,
901-767-8930,
memorialparkfuneralandcemetery.com

PLAY ARCHAEOLOGIST
AT CHUCALISSA

C.H. Nash Museum/Chucalissa Archaeological Site

Before Elvis—heck, before Hernando de Soto—American Indians settled this area. We know this, in part, because Civilian Conservation Corps laborers digging a pool for T.O. Fuller State Park in the 1930s unearthed their village, a mound complex that peaked around 1500 A.D.

The mounds are cool. What impresses me most, however, is the site's archives, packed with finds from years of excavation, and the openness of Chucalissa's staff: These people want you, and even your kids, to get hands-on processing prehistoric artifacts.

After a year of honing, Chucalissa reopened its Archaeology Lab in the spring of 2016. Retooled lab + backlog of artifacts = more hands-on opportunity than ever, so plan to spend about an hour playing archaeologist before checking out the site's other improvements, including exhibits upgraded with help from the Chickasaw Nation and the Mississippi Band of Choctaw. Lab "shifts" run on Saturdays year-round; summertime adds shifts on Tuesdays and Thursdays.

While on-site, follow the half-mile nature trail through an arboretum to points within T.O. Fuller State Park, spying for surprises like a Walden-esque writing desk tucked in the woods.

C.H. Nash Museum/Chucalissa Archaeological Site, 1987 Indian Village Dr., 901-785-3160, memphis.edu/chucalissa *Closed Monday*

T.O. Fuller State Park, 1500 Mitchell Rd., 901-543-7581, tnstateparks.com/parks/about/t-o-fuller

LEARN FREE

Pink Palace Museum

If you're in the Mid-South and want to see a shrunken head, a miniature circus, and other relics of Memphis gone-by, you go to the Pink Palace Museum. Since Edition 1 of this book, however, Memphis's "attic" has been updating. In 2014, its IMAX theater went 3D digital. In 2016, its planetarium went full-dome digital. (I didn't know what that meant either 'til the planetarium manager swiped something on his tablet and I went hurtling through the Kuiper Belt. Apparently the new software can generate simulations of the cosmos like that.) By summer 2016, the Pink Palace mansion and exhibit buildings will begin closing, one at a time, for additional upgrades. Don't worry: The IMAX theater and planetarium will remain open throughout, and your shrunken head and miniature circus will endure. They'll just be moved from the exhibit building into the mansion, along with the replica Piggly Wiggly. (If you don't know, the first self-service grocery was founded by Memphian Clarence Saunders and the Pink Palace mansion was, sort of, his home.)

Here's the free part: Year-round on Tuesdays, 1 p.m. to close, admission is free to the Pink Palace. The museum also offers free summer membership. Look for details on the museum website around May.

3050 Central Ave., 901-636-2362,
memphismuseums.org

TIME-TRAVEL
IN COLLIERVILLE

Morton Museum of Collierville History

Collierville sits 30 minutes southeast of Memphis, but can feel centuries removed considering its ornamental cannons, preserved churches, and postcard of a town square. Start at the Morton Museum of Collierville History, a pocket of exhibits inside circa-1873 Collierville Christian Church (free admission). Before you leave, enter the former sanctuary, glorious with stained glass and spindles, and inquire into two brochures: one that points you to the preserved exteriors of four additional churches within walking distance; the other, Collierville's Civil War Walking Tour, a compact route blazed by interpretive signs detailing the 1863 Battle of Collierville, and how General William Tecumseh Sherman nearly incinerated the town. Listen as you tramp for the rhythmic railing of the train and the random chiming of "Amazing Grace."

196 N. Main St., Collierville, 901-457-2650,
colliervillemuseum.org
Closed Sunday and Monday

THEN,
SQUARE UP

Collierville Town Square

You've trekked past Collierville's historic churches and Civil War sites. You're hungry and wondering what's with the railcars lined up downtown. Regroup on the Square, a spoil of green space, benches, bike racks, public restrooms, and shops fringed by free parking and those vintage railcars. The cars are open Monday through Friday; don't miss the hat racks and tiny kitchen of the 1940s-era "executive" railcar. As you step off, window and sidewalk displays lure you to shop for anything from cowboy boots to jewelry, and you can nab lunch and a cup of regionally crafted Sweet Magnolia gelato at Square Beans. Better yet? Take dessert to go and enjoy it on one of those benches I mentioned with a view to Collierville's Main Street, voted "America's Best" by *Parade* magazine readers in 2014.

Main Street Collierville
(for additional information on the Square),
125 N. Rowlett St., Collierville, 901-853-1666,
mainstreetcollierville.org
Closed Saturday and Sunday

Square Beans
103 N. Center St., Collierville, 901-854-8855,
squarebeans.com
Closed most Sundays

Paunika Jones and Kevin Thomas of Collage Dance Collective, page 36. Photo credit: Andrew Breig.

THE ARTS
(AND ARTFUL SOUVENIRS)

Memphis is such a cradle for creativity, this section covers everything from visual and performing arts to books and films. Our city is a fine place to be in an audience, but Memphis begs you to do more than sit back and watch. Our art and artists are accessible: They'll meet you in unexpected places and, sometimes, encourage you to jump right in. Memphis's wide creative space nurtures makers, too, so we'll discuss where to find their wares, which make infinitely cooler souvenirs than mass-produced t-shirts anyway.

SMILE FOR
AMURICA

Jamie Harmon's Amurica photo booth and studio

If there's one souvenir photo you need of Memphis, it's a portrait inside the Amurica photo booth. Freelance photographer Jamie Harmon fashioned the original booth in 2011 by bedazzling the interior of a 1959 silver teardrop trailer with string lights and choose-your-own props: wigs, sunglasses, masks, baby dolls, a plastic goat. Since then, he's opened a studio and added photo booth trailers: two mobile, one stationary, both exquisitely out-there. When the booths aren't rented for private events, Harmon and friends park them around town and host periodic in-studio events, when you can sit for a portrait or pile in the photo booth with pals and take home a print for a fee.

410 N. Cleveland St., 901-606-2041,
amurica.com

GET A LOAD
OF *THIS* BROAD

Broad Avenue Arts District

This Broad is Broad Avenue, where technicolor murals and ashy industrial sites lay out like a funky charm bracelet. Get to know her by:

Choosing Memphis-made souvenirs. There's no greater concentration of shops representing Memphis artists and makers than Broad Avenue. Stock up on tees, jewelry, and art prints at Five in One Social Club and Falling into Place.

Art-walking. One spring evening and again in fall, crowds spill from Broad's businesses into a street party. These Art Walks are ideal for meeting local creators, say, mezzo-fresco artist Tom Clifton at his gallery, T. Clifton Art, or popping in on an artist's reception at Found Memphis. Follow broadavearts.com or individual businesses for details.

Dancing. Dance on Broad events start as informal dance lessons and end as all-out dance parties (free admission; fall months). Whether the theme is Bollywood or line dancing, the groove is in moving with the crowd beneath Broad's colorful Water Tower Pavilion, a loading dock that transforms into a gathering space on weekends.

Patronizing public art. In Edition 1 of this book, I pointed you to the mural by French street artist Remed, not that you could miss it. Since then, Broad's welcomed additional projects, from the paint job on the aforementioned water tower to the I Love Memphis mural at Scott Street.

Dining, page 79; **drinking**, page 95; and **listening to live music**, page 128.

The Broad Avenue Arts District is loosely defined by
North Hollywood Street, Broad Avenue,
Collins Street, and Sam Cooper Boulevard.

Falling into Place
2613 Broad Ave., 901-249-2834,
fallingintoplace.net
Closed Monday

Five in One Social Club
2535 Broad Ave., 901-308-2104,
fiveinone.org
Closed Monday

Found Memphis
2491 Broad Ave., 901-607-1328,
foundmemphis.com
Closed Monday

T. Clifton Art
2571 Broad Ave., 901-323-2787,
tcliftonart.com
Closed Sunday and Monday

Water Tower Pavilion
2542 Broad Ave.,
broadavearts.com

BONUS:
7 STEPS TO DIY SOUVENIRS

I'm focusing on open-studio and workshop opportunities here, but all of these businesses keep regular hours to feed your Pinterest board and retail cravings. Contact each for details.

1. The Art Project. You could register young ones for classes from woodworking to fashion design at this creative studio for kids. My 8-year-old prefers to drop in. For $12, she gets 90 minutes of "art free play" to do things with glitter and tempera I'd never allow at home. I get to hang close by, assisting as needed, but mostly scribbling in an adult coloring book while nursing a beer (available for purchase at the counter). *2092 Trimble Pl., 901-425-3434, artprojectmemphis.com; closed Monday and for periodic private parties*

2/3. Bumbletees Sewing Studio and **Sew Memphis.** These pretty-as-a-picture fabric boutiques host hand- and machine-sewing classes for adults and kids. Check each store's class calendar to decide what you'll make, from A-line skirts to laptop sleeves. *Bumbletees Sewing Studio, 2219 S. Germantown Rd., Germantown, 901-755-9701, bumbletees.wordpress.com; Sew Memphis, 2075 Madison Ave., #6, 901-244-6224, sewmemphis.com*

4. Falling into Place. Mary Claire White began selling her candles at Five in One Social Club on Broad Avenue before opening her own shop/studio, Falling into Place, down the street. In her workshop, you'll wick, mix fragrances, pour wax, and make labels for two clean-burning, long-lasting soy candles. *2613 Broad Ave., 901-249-2834, fallingintoplace.net*

5. Five in One Social Club. Behind Five in One's gift shop is a workshop space that owner Alice Laskey-Castle calls "kindergarten for grown folks." Difference here is that you can BYOB and chit-chat all you want with your classmates. Check the workshop calendar for offerings such as Wine Bottle Wednesdays, when you can turn empty wine bottles into wine tumblers. *2535 Broad Ave., 901-308-2104, fiveinone.org*

6. Me and Mrs. Jones. Want to learn how to upcycle furniture? Study under Stephanie Jones, whose artisanal paint techniques can make any old thing look fabulous. Floral design workshops, too. *889 S. Cooper St., 901-494-8786, and 2135 Merchant's Row, #4, Germantown, 901-604-8846; mrsjonespaintedfinishes.com*

7. Metal Museum. Even with no experience, you can blacksmith, weld, and cast at the country's only museum dedicated to metal art and craft, page 41. So go ahead: Forge a bottle opener, a bracelet, or, better yet, a set of barbecuing tools—this *is* Memphis. *374 Metal Museum Dr., 901-774-6380, metalmuseum.org*

STUDY
THE MEMPHIS MASTERS

Memphis Brooks Museum of Art

Traveling exhibitions will vie for your attention at the Memphis Brooks Museum of Art, so focus for me: Take one day to study the Memphis Masters of photography: Ernest Withers, page 50, and William Eggleston. The Brooks's permanent collection favors these men who lived and worked in Memphis: Withers documenting the civil rights era in moments; Eggleston turning the everyday into the arresting through his lens. If you read Edition 1 of this book, you knew to look for these images—nearly 500 of them—in the museum lobby, where they were displayed two at a time, one for each photographer.

In May 2016, the Brooks will begin throwing itself a year-long centennial birthday bash. Throughout the party, you'll be invited to enjoy special museum exhibits, outdoor installations, a new hands-on gallery for families, and greater exposure to Withers and Eggleston: As a centennial gift, Memphis's masters of photography are moving into a dedicated gallery.

Memphis Brooks Museum of Art is located inside Overton Park at
1934 Poplar Ave., 901-544-6200,
brooksmuseum.org
Closed Monday and Tuesday

COME TO
CROSSTOWN

Crosstown Concourse and Crosstown Arts

Navigate to the address below and, depending on your timing, you'll either see a construction zone or a vision achieved. In the youth of its first life (1927–1993), the complex at 495 N. Watkins St. bustled with shoppers and employees as a Sears, Roebuck & Company distribution center and retail store. Act two is anticipated for 2017, a recasting of the 1.5-million-square-foot structure as living space, artist studios, forums for creative programming (see note), headquarters for some of Memphis's most innovative nonprofits, and a branch of Kimbal Musk's family of real-food cafés.

Note: Crosstown Arts is the right-brain behind this programming. They'll move to Crosstown Concourse when construction's complete. Until then, find them at 422 and 430 N. Watkins St., where they host a mix of unjuried and curated displays of visual and performing arts, including shows by their own artists-in-residence. Check the calendar at crosstownarts.org for details.

---

495 N. Watkins St.,
crosstownconcourse.com

DANCE TO
A DIFFERENT BEAT

Collage Dance Collective and New Ballet Ensemble & School

Maybe you've seen *The Nutcracker.* Maybe you've even seen it habitually, like a winter-holiday tradition on repeat. Take the needle off the record: Unless you've seen New Ballet Ensemble's *Nut ReMix,* you've never seen it like this. There will be tutus. There may even be live accompaniment, thanks to the Memphis Symphony Orchestra. But there will also be African drumming and dancing. A hip-hop battle. A number that grooves to "Green Onions." And jookin', that Memphis style of street dance that makes its practitioners look fluid from their rippling hand movements down to their sneakers. This might sound like stylistic whiplash, but taken together, it's anything but; rather, *Nut ReMix* shows what dance can be, and that it brings people together. It's no surprise then that the White House recognized New Ballet in 2014 with a National Arts and Humanities Youth Program Award.

Catch *Nut ReMix* the weekend before Thanksgiving. If you like what you see, get to New Ballet Ensemble's eclectic *Springloaded* show in April, and watch for performances by Collage Dance Collective. Collage is newer to Memphis but no less committed; as I was researching for this edition, several professional dancers had just moved from cities around the world to grow the company. Every performance manifests Collage's charge to foster diversity in ballet: Students and professionals dance together, classical and contemporary techniques fuse, and choreography makes a statement.

Collage Dance Collective
2497 Broad Ave., 901-800-1873,
collagedance.org

New Ballet Ensemble & School
2157 York Ave., 901-726-9225,
newballet.org

CELEBRATE
THE DIXON'S 40TH

Dixon Gallery & Gardens

Dixon Gallery & Gardens marks its 40th year in 2016, yet the gifts are all for you:

Tuesday admission is still pay what you wish; don't miss the free gallery tour at 2 p.m.

Saturday admission, 10 a.m.–noon, is free, including Family Studio art-making activities (first Saturdays monthly).

A new on-site café, Park & Cherry, debuted under the direction of chefs Wally Joe and Andrew Adams of Memphis's ACRE Restaurant.

In sum, it'll be easier than ever to while away a day among the Dixon's permanent and changing exhibits, and across its 17-acre grounds. Take your time therein to discover garden rooms just as the late Hugo Dixon planned them, receive a shady reminder of the Dixon's arboretum status, and come upon allées and statuary commissioned by the Dixon family.

4339 Park Ave., 901-761-5250,
dixon.org
Closed Monday

GET TO
THIS HOUSE PARTY

GLITCH Gallery

Adam Farmer is a painter, assemblage artist, and curator of his living room. Over a series of once-a-month shows, the space has been covered in tinfoil by Jill Wissmiller, painted by Derrick Dent and Birdcap, and masked by mirrors and frenetic geometric patterns courtesy of Lance Turner.

Whether Farmer books a band or the featured artist(s) weave in a performance element, to step inside GLITCH is to be cocooned in a den of sight and sound. Maybe this isn't what you do in your living room, but this is how Farmer feels at home, cozied up in a hybrid of art forms.

Before you leave, walk through the kitchen, where an Alex Warble painting warms the stove, to the backyard. Farmer's created a sculpture garden here, a series of shrine-y stations layered with collected objects and the debris of nature.

2180 Cowden Ave.,
facebook.com/glitchery

SCREEN
AN INDIE

Indie Memphis

If you only know Indie Memphis for its November film festival, that's a start. Nearing its 20th anniversary, the festival is more successful than ever, spilling from Overton Square, page 44, into the South Main Historic Arts District, page 46. Likewise, Indie Memphis's programming is spilling beyond November into every single month of your calendar with a clear mission: to connect local filmmakers with resources, and to give local audiences the choice to see films of merit, outside the mainstream, that they can't see anywhere else in Memphis. Watch for:

• Free monthly events at Crosstown Arts, page 35, including MicroCinema evenings, which present curated, themed blocks of short films

• Monthly screenings of indies and classics (weekly during Memphis in May, the annual citywide celebration of ourselves and a featured country)

• The Soul Cinema series at the Stax Museum of American Soul Music, page 116

• Special screenings when Memphis directors release new projects outside of festival time

If you love a cinephile, or you love yourself and you're a cinephile, Indie Memphis memberships are $50 and regale you with all sorts of exclusives and discounts.

indiememphis.com

VISIT
THE COUNTRY'S METAL MUSEUM

Metal Museum

Rooftops and riverboats make pretty perches for ogling the Mississippi River. But to my eye, the Metal Museum unfurls it best: near a bend in the river that creates angles unlike the head-on vista you get just north in downtown; shrouded by mystic trees, a sculpture garden, and architecture with a story. Go for any museum event—late September's annual Repair Days are popular, but most Saturdays and Sundays at 2:30 and 3 p.m., you can witness forging and casting demos that remind you that this is a working museum alive with an artist-in-residence and apprentices (and, ahem, it's the only institution in the U.S. devoted to metal art and craft). Before or after the demos, view permanent and rotating exhibits in the galleries and browse the gift shop, which expanded in 2014. Inspired? Come back to take a class, page 33.

Come back to take a class, page 33.

374 Metal Museum Dr., 901-774-6380,
metalmuseum.org
Closed Monday

#FREEOPERA

Opera Memphis's 30 Days of Opera

Think you hate opera? Not in Memphis you don't. Since 2012, Opera Memphis has surprised the city by popping up and belting it out at the dog park, the farmers market, the library—wherever—during its annual 30 Days of Opera series, usually planned for September. Some of the appearances are published in advance; others you'll have to crack via social media, or just listen for the trill.

Caveat: 30 Days of Opera may be something of a gateway drug, considering that Opera Memphis Director Ned Canty is the guy who reworked *The Mikado* to star Godzilla and Pikachu. You've been warned.

Oh, and if you're around in spring instead of fall, seek out the Midtown Opera Festival. Centered around Playhouse on the Square, page 44, this week-plus of events includes fully staged operas, world premieres of opera originals, family shows, and talks.

6745 Wolf River Pkwy., 901-257-3100,
operamemphis.org

GO BACKSTAGE
AT THE ORPHEUM

The Orpheum Theatre

There are tons of historic and ornamental details to process at The Orpheum Theatre (literally: The Czechoslovakian chandeliers in the auditorium weigh 2,000 pounds apiece). Let Brett Batterson, The Orpheum's new president and CEO, talk you through the theater's history from its origins in 1890 as the Grand Opera House. It'll cost you (around $75 for non-subscribers), but periodic Dinner on Stage events get you cocktails and a three-course meal with Batterson. Afterward, you'll shadow him on a guided tour of the theater, which reveals 200-and-counting backstage murals created by visiting casts and crews since The Orpheum's 1996–97 season.

203 S. Main St., 901-525-3000,
orpheum-memphis.com

GIVE
A STANDING O

Overton Square Theater District

With live music venues and enough restaurants to feed two weeks' worth of date nights, Overton Square is an instant night out. Guess what? It's Memphis's theater district, too, staging a mix of familiar shows and homegrown originals. In 1975, Playhouse on the Square moved in. Today, its resident professionals, plus a cast of others, star in productions at three Overton Square venues: TheatreWorks, the Circuit, and Playhouse on the Square. In 2014, Memphis's black repertory theater, Hattiloo, relocated from the edge of downtown Memphis to Overton Square in a new, but intimate as ever, space. It's *the* regional venue to cycle through pioneers like August Wilson and encounter works by Memphis playwrights Katori Hall and Hattiloo founder Ekundayo Bandele.

P.S. Wondering what's with the construction at North Cooper Street and Madison Avenue? That's Ballet Memphis's latest space going in. balletmemphis.org

---

The Circuit Playhouse, 51 S. Cooper St., 901-726-4656,
playhouseonthesquare.org

Hattiloo Theatre, 37 S. Cooper St., 901-525-0009,
hattiloo.org

Playhouse on the Square, 66 S. Cooper St., 901-726-4656,
playhouseonthesquare.org

TheatreWorks, 2085 Monroe Ave., 901-274-7139,
theatreworksmemphis.org

STUMBLE ON
THIS CELEB PHOTOGRAPHER

Robinson Gallery

Jack Robinson photographed everyone who was anyone in 1960s fashion and pop culture. He worked for the magazines and newspapers everyone was reading: *Life, Vogue,* the *New York Times.* Yet he lived the latter part of his life quietly in Memphis. So quietly, in fact, the city wasn't wholly clued into his body of work until after his death. Ask a staff member at Robinson Gallery to relate the story, then survey the photographer's black-and-white celebrity portraits and neon-charged streetscapes on two levels of exhibit space.

Exclusive for my readers: Buy the gallery's coffee table book of Robinson's work and the staff will include an 8x8 print: your choice of Joni Mitchell, Jack Nicholson, the Who, or Tina Turner (she's from West Tennessee, you know).

400 S. Front St., 901-576-0708,
robinsongallery.com
Closed Saturday and Sunday, except by appointment

SOAK UP
SOUTH MAIN

South Main Historic Arts District

This district and its defining thoroughfare, South Main Street, bridge the historic and the current. Amid splashes of public art, century-old facades nurture enterprising creatives and a surging residential population. Together, these elements create an energy and familial feeling you'll dig as you . . .

Stock up on Memphis-made fashion. There's no way I'm letting you leave Memphis with a soul-less souvenir. T-shirts boldly interpreting Memphis's landmarks and vibe are sketched and printed on-site at Sachë; local designers, including Quistt, who crafts necklaces and clutches in African prints, stock K'PreSha.

Experience Trolley Night. During this street party on South Main (final Fridays monthly, 6–9 p.m.), businesses open their doors wide, pour drinks, and host surprises from art showings to live music, including songwriter sets at South Main Sounds. Follow gosouthmain.com or "Meet Me in Memphis" on Facebook for details.

Return for RiverArtsFest. If you're down for a weekend-long artsy street party, get to October's RiverArtsFest, when artist booths stretch for blocks down South Main Street (live music and food trucks, too).

Art-walk. Follow the South Main Mosaic Art Walk to eight temporary installations of public art. Linger at stop 4: Those people-sized flowers sculpted by the Metal Museum, page 41, signal a lawn for bocce ball. Check out equipment from neighboring businesses.

Hang out for history, pages 13-15; **music**, pages 109 and 124; **food**, starting on page 79; and/or **nightlife**, page 125.

K'PreSha
323 S. Main St.,
901-249-4986,
kpreshaboutique.com

RiverArtsFest
riverartsmemphis.org

Saché
525 S. Main St.,
901-922-5549,
sachedesign.com

South Main Sounds
550 S. Main St.

DRIVE IN

Time Warp Movie Series at the Summer Drive-In

Mike McCarthy is passionate about preserving American institutions, and he's passionate about films (he's made several through his Guerilla Monster production company). He fuses his passions, with help from Matt Martin of Memphis's The Black Lodge, into the Time Warp Movie Series at the Summer Drive-In. For its part, the drive-in is deliciously old-school, one of McCarthy's beloved institutions that turns 50 in 2016. When it's Time Warp time, the drive-in screens four films from dusk to dawn. The cult and classic selections dive into a different theme each month, say, monsterama. On such a night, you could burrow in your vehicle, gorging on gothic horror and popcorn. But McCarthy bets you'll be captivated by the screen *and* the scene: Walk to the concession stand. Meet other Time Warpers and chat about movies or how incredible it is that Memphis still has this drive-in theater. That's McCarthy's vision of "free-range cinema."

The Time Warp Movie Series goes down one weekend evening a month, several months throughout the year. Outside of the series, hit the Summer Drive-In for new releases.

5310 Summer Ave., 901-767-4320,
facebook.com/timewarpdrivein

RUMMAGE
IN STYLE

Urban Barn Market

What glamping is to camping, Urban Barn Market is to flea-marketing. Rather than tunneling your way through labyrinthine stalls of indiscriminate hoards, you'll stroll through cover-shoot-ready vignettes of artful antiques, vintage décor, and handcrafted pieces. Each of the approximately 45 vendors is personally selected by market creators Debi Heying Vincent and Carrie Walters Floyd, so the roster reads like a best-of Memphis makers (Melissa Bridgman's perfectly imperfect pottery always makes me smile).

Bonus: Urban Barn's bi-annual markets pop up in locations with aesthetic value of their own. The Mother's Day weekend market traditionally fills the interior, grounds, and carriage house of the historic Woodruff-Fontaine House, page 16, for example. Anticipate a second market just before the winter holidays.

urbanbarnmarketmemphis.com

LOOK THROUGH
ERNEST WITHERS'S LENS

Withers Collection Museum & Gallery

Among individual photographers covering the U.S. civil rights movement, Ernest Withers is commonly credited with producing the vastest body of work. Before his death, Withers told his daughter Rosalind that his portfolio was five million images strong. She stopped counting a few years back at one million. The highlights hang inside the Withers Collection Museum & Gallery, a Beale Street storefront that housed Withers's studio. There is happiness here: Negro League baseball portraits, two would-be kings (B.B. and Elvis) smiling. And there is a heaviness: bus boycotts, protests, and school desegregation documented; graphic stills taken moments after the murders of Emmett Till and Martin Luther King Jr. You may need an hour to see the collection and many more to process what you've seen.

333 Beale St., 901-523-2344,
thewitherscollection.com
Closed Monday

SPILL IT

Spillit Memphis

Once upon a time, Memphian Leah T. Keys tuned into *The Moth Radio Hour* and marveled at how connected she felt to its storytellers, despite her geographic distance. Wondering what the stories were in her own city, she built Spillit, Memphis's own true storytelling platform.

Once or twice a month, storytellers and listeners pack into Amurica, page 29, for two varieties of Spillit events. For periodic Center Stage events, storytellers are selected in advance and given 10 minutes to present workshopped stories. For near-monthly Slams, anyone can throw their name in the bucket upon arrival; storytellers are selected at random and given six minutes to spill it. All events are themed, from Coming Out to Adventures and Travels, and Slam events are judged, culminating in a Grand Slam featuring the year's winners. For any event, arrive early; seating is limited.

Whether or not you take the stage, Keys wants you to know that listeners are as important as storytellers here. For what value does a person's story have without someone to listen and connect to it, even if the parties are strangers?

spillitmemphis.org

BONUS:
5 MORE SCENES FOR STORY-SEEKERS

1. Benjamin L. Hooks Central Library. If you fall in the 13- to 18-year-old set, ditch your parents and enter CLOUD901. (For real: No parents allowed.) Even without a Memphis Public Library card, teens can join free scheduled events from sketch mobs in the art studio to music production workshops in the teched-out control room. Workshop registration may be required, so check memphislibrary.org/cloud901 before you go. With younger children, listen for periodic Family Tunes & Tales events at Central Library and satellite branches. These Saturday morning presentations combine storytelling with live music from the Memphis Symphony Orchestra and a craft. *Central Library, 3030 Poplar Ave., is open daily with the exception of CLOUD901, which is closed Friday. Visit memphislibrary.org for more information, including satellite locations and hours.*

2. The Booksellers at Laurelwood. If you're looking for a bookstore where you can stay all day, this is it. The Booksellers Bistro serves breakfast, lunch, and dinner; cushy chairs invite you to curl up; and the calendar's covered with events from book signings to Miss Marjorie's story hour for children (Tuesdays and Thursdays at 11 a.m.). *387 Perkins Extd., 901-683-9801, thebooksellersatlaurelwood.com*

3. Burke's Book Store. A visit to Burke's, established in 1875, is as much about thumbing through new and second-hand books as it is about conversing with the staff. Ask owner Corey Mesler for his poem of the week; talk screenwriting with associate David Tankersley. Leave a thank-you note using one of the vintage typewriters tucked into the store's alcoves. *936 S. Cooper St., 901-278-7484, burkesbooks.com*

4. Mid-South Book Festival. Annually in September, this festival brings conferences for student and adult writers, author panels and signings, and a book-happy street fair to Memphis's Overton Square and Cooper-Young neighborhoods. *midsouthbookfest.org*

5. Storybooth. Storybooth is a coordinator of student writing workshops, host of talks and signings by local and visiting authors, and a pocket-sized bookstore. Then a staffer tugs on a bookshelf, revealing a high-ceilinged room with tomes shelved top to bottom. Surprise: Storybooth is also a lending library for the entire family. *438 N. Cleveland St., 901-573-8444, crosstownarts.org/story-booth; hours vary*

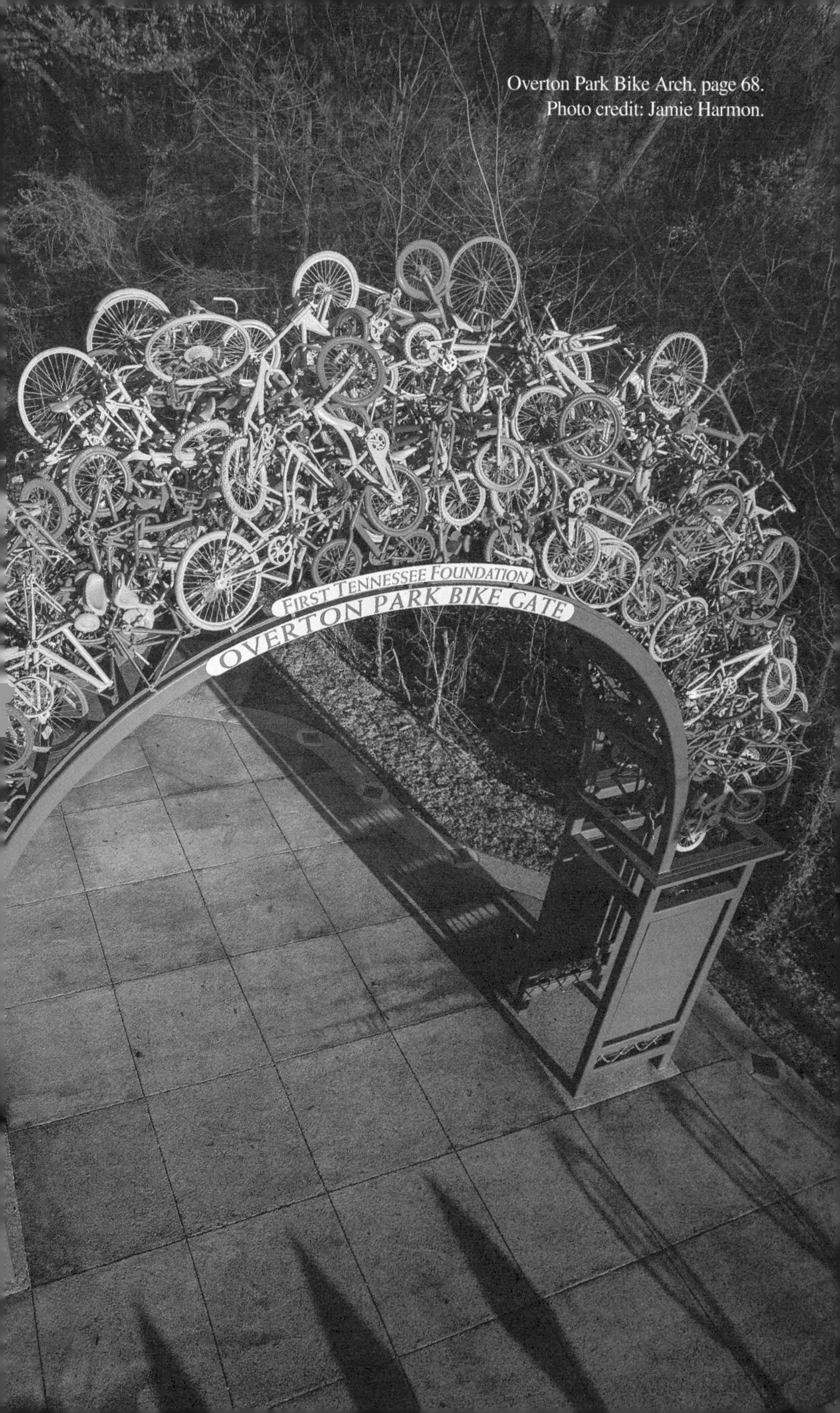

Overton Park Bike Arch, page 68.
Photo credit: Jamie Harmon.

SPORTS AND RECREATION

If you're looking for ways to walk off your Memphis calories, they're here. Over the following pages, you'll learn how to stitch together a Mississippi River run/walk and connect to our expanding bike trails. But Memphis surprises. So you'll also discover where to hike an old-growth forest in the middle of the city, where to do yoga in a brewery, and where to tire your kids the heck out (in the most inventive ways). And because there's nothing like being wrapped up in the blue-and-gold cloak of exhilaration that is Grizzlies season in Memphis, we'll talk about spectator sports, too.

Grit and grind, y'all.

ROLL UP
ON A GRIZZ PARTY

Tour de Grizz

Tour de Grizz is a group bike ride from the Memphis Zoo, home of grizzly bears, to the FedEx Forum, home of the NBA Memphis Grizzlies, and back. Historically, the ride rolls in March or April, usually coinciding with the Grizzlies' last regular season home game, though you might catch the 2016 ride in fall. Your registration fee includes zoo admission, participation in the ride, a ticket to the evening's Grizzlies game, and bike valet at the zoo and the Forum. The 10-mile round-trip ride is magic: It's you in a parade of spandexed road warriors, parents pulling babies in bike trailers, and kids who've just learned to ride. The Memphis Police Department shuts down major thoroughfares just for you, then escorts you through neighborhoods and back roads to downtown. By the time you roll up, the party will already be in progress outside FedEx Forum. Listen to the beat of the Grizzlies Drumline in the shadow of Beale Street and anticipate the NBA electricity that awaits inside.

grizzlies.com

Need a bike while you're in town? See page 59.

CYCLE
THE COUNTRY'S MOST IMPROVED BIKE CITY

Bike trails and rentals

In Edition 1 of this book, the Bike Trails and Rentals page went something like this:

It wasn't long ago that Memphis was shamed for its unfriendliness toward cyclists. In a speedy turn facilitated by the city and grassroots groups, the movement got wheels, carving bike lanes and rails-to-trails—and earning that "most improved" nod from *Bicycling* magazine.

Fast-forward to 2016 and the Shelby Farms Greenline, the pioneering, 6.5-mile corridor paved through the heart of the city to Shelby Farms Park, page 71, has grown at both ends. Its western terminus now links to Overton Park, pages 67–68, via a two-mile protected path called the Hampline; its eastern end stretches 4.5 miles east from Shelby Farms Park into Old Cordova.

Pick up the Shelby Farms Greenline from either of these new entrées, or:

• from Shelby Farms Park, page 71, shelbyfarmspark.org/shelbyfarmsgreenline

• at access points mid-route. In particular, Highland Street, High Point Terrace, Graham Street, Waring Road, and Podesta Street provide street parking within neighborhoods and shorten the route in case you're no endurance racer.

Need a bike while you're in town? Rent one at Shelby Farms Park, or contact one of these local bike shops for a rental:

- All About Bikes, 621 S. Mendenhall Rd., 901-767-6240, allaboutbikesllc.com
- Midtown Bike Company, 517 S. Main St., 901-522-9757, midtownbikecompany.com
- Peddler Bike Shop Memphis, 3548 Walker Ave., 901-327-4833, peddlerbikeshop.com
- Revolutions Bicycle Cooperative, page 70

Need a map? A new map of bike lanes, off-road trails, and protected paths is available at most bike shops. You can also view and order it here: memphistravel.com/memphis-bike-map

PLAY
INDOORS AND OUT

Children's Museum of Memphis

I warned you in Edition 1 of this book:

Do not pass the Children's Museum of Memphis (CMOM) with children unless you're prepared to stop. The technicolor exterior, intensified by the 2013 addition of a splash pad, grabs kids' attention like a paper wand grabs spun sugar.

The situation has intensified.

In late 2014, CMOM replaced its front parking lot with a play space that's compact but innovative. The equipment, largely boundary-free, has newfangled names, but the essence is classic: Saddle Spinners are akin to personal merry-go-rounds that kids power by shifting their weight; the We-Saw is a wheelchair-friendly teeter-totter; the ZipKrooz, a two-way zip line that mists riders in warm weather. To my relief, there are several layers of padding beneath the Astroturf ground that soften monkey-bar spills, and fans and shade tents that pop up in summer.

The play space, designed for 5- to 12-year-olds, is open year-round, as is a scaled-down version located inside for kids ages 4 and under.

Back outside, the splash pad gurgles Memorial Day through Labor Day. Play inside and out on a $20 combo ticket; save money by bringing your own snacks and lunch to the picnic area surrounding the splash pad.

2525 Central Ave., 901-458-2678,
cmom.com

GET HOOPY

Co-Motion Studio

If a business could be powered by unicorns and rainbows, this studio, whose name suggests a "community in motion," is it. Owners Chloe Evans and Adriene Holland, along with guest instructors, teach regular classes in yoga, parkour, and hula-hooping for a variety of ages and experience levels. So even if you've never dropped-and-rolled off an obstacle or picked up a hoop, you can aspire to be a parkour star or free-flowing hoop-dancer (glowsticks optional).

If Co-Motion's class schedule doesn't match yours, stop by on Sundays for Hoop Church, a pay-what-you-can, play-what-you-can movement/instrument circle. Before you leave, shop the studio's retail collection for a hoop made with love by Chloe and Adriene.

416 N. Cleveland St., 901-316-7733,
comotionmemphis.com
Hours vary

PADDLE
THE WOLF

Ghost River Outfitters

If the Wolf River you know intersects Mississippi River industry, you're wondering why I'm telling you to do this. It's because I want you to head east about 50 miles to Moscow, Tennessee, where the Wolf is all cypress trees and grassy islands and forested walls, thanks in part to advocacy efforts by the Wolf River Conservancy. Mid-March through mid-November, Ghost River Outfitters will hook you up with a canoe, kayak, or stand-up paddleboard, life vests, and paddles to explore the upper Wolf. Call ahead and Mark Babb and crew will have your gear ready whether you want to rent by the hour (weekends from noon 'til sunset), commission guide service, or run the Ghost, the primordial section of the Wolf that flows through five ecosystems in eight miles. Babb's Ghost River run takes 3 to 5 hours by kayak ($40) or 4 to 6 hours by canoe ($50) and includes shuttle service and gear.

901-485-1220,
ghostriverrentals.com

HANG WITH
A NATURALIST

Meeman-Shelby Forest State Park

Memorial Day through Labor Day, Meeman-Shelby Forest State Park adds at least one seasonal naturalist to its staff. Translation: More fun for you. Offerings vary annually; my family's stumbled upon activities from hands-on reptile programs to pontoon boat rides around the park's Poplar Tree Lake, where red-eared sliders sun on logs and some 200 bird species fly overhead. Our favorite seasonal activity is the guided paddle on the park's Eagle Lake, a swamp where towering cypress trees create shady outdoor rooms.

Tip: Visiting outside of these months? Meeman-Shelby Forest State Park is quieter, cooler, and abloom in early spring with snow-white dogwoods, lavender phlox, and stands of sunny wildflowers.

910 Riddick Rd., Millington, 901-876-5215,
tnstateparks.com/parks/about/meeman-shelby

FALL
FOR THIS MAZE

Mid-South Corn Maze

You know it's fall in Memphis when mums wage an occupation of front porches, Gibson's brings back the pumpkin doughnut, and the Mid-South Maze materializes amid the cornstalks of Agricenter International. Plan at least an hour to conquer the maze; "corn cops" stationed throughout provide guidance if you need it. Though the course changes annually, it's known for letting its Memphis show: The 2015 maze rendered Grizzlies center Marc Gasol in corn-stalk relief.

The maze opens around mid-September for approximately eight weeks. Bring cash or check, and plan to spend a little extra on auxiliary activities: joining a haunted hayride, bouncing on the jumping pillow, and launching ears of corn from a cannon. Seriously.

7777 Walnut Grove Rd., 901-870-6338,
midsouthmaze.com

GET
RIVERFIT

Mississippi Riverfront parks

String together these downtown parks and landmarks for a workout with a view. I'm providing exact locations for the start and finish points; for maps to points in between, visit memphisriverfront.com.

1. Start on the south end of downtown in quiet Martyrs Park. (If you're lost, navigate to 803 Channel 3 Drive; it's basically next door.)

2. Head northeast to Tom Lee Park, where you can battle the overhead bars and log chin-ups at RiverFit, a battery of fitness stations. Don't miss stairwells painted with the Memphis Grizzlies' mantra, "grit and grind," across Riverside Drive. *getriverfit.com*

3. Continue northeast along the river, using Beale Street Landing, page 10, the historic cobblestones, and Mississippi River Park as waymarkers.

4. Beyond Mississippi River Park, the route turns concrete jungle for a stretch. Pass the Tennessee Welcome Center, go around the back of Bass Pro Shops at the Pyramid, page 10, and connect to Front Street. Keep working northeast to reach the A.W. Willis Bridge. Cross it, stopping at its crest to admire the river.

5. Over the bridge, hook north to Mississippi River Greenbelt Park, anchored by mammoth trees. (The park is located along Island Drive between the A.W. Willis Bridge and North Mud Island Road.)

Congrats. Depending on how intricate you got with your route, you likely logged between 3.5 and 5 miles. Double back—you know you want to see it all again.

RUN WILD
IN THIS BACKYARD

My Big Backyard at Memphis Botanic Garden

I could list several grown-up reasons for you to visit Memphis Botanic Garden: wine tastings, workshops, concerts. You should do those. But with kids, you should do one thing: Go wild in My Big Backyard, a progressive playground where young'uns pinball around 13 different vignettes across 2.5 acres. They'll squeal over rushing through a rainbow of playhouses, tunneling through wormholes, dancing in the (automated) rain, hula-hooping on the lawn, climbing into a kid-sized birdhouse, and constructing log forts; you'll squeal over tiring them out. Admission to My Big Backyard is included with Memphis Botanic Garden admission.

Outside of My Big Backyard, two other Memphis Botanic Garden landscapes are natural kid-pleasers: Buy food at the reception desk to feed koi in the Japanese Garden; lead future paleontologists to the Prehistoric Garden, where they can uncover fossils in a sandy dig pit surrounded by ferns and magnolias.

750 Cherry Rd., 901-636-4100,
memphisbotanicgarden.com

HIKE AN OLD FOREST
IN THE HEART OF THE CITY

Overton Park's Old Forest

Think of Overton Park's Old Forest, officially designated the Old Forest State Natural Area in 2011, as your personal forest—smack in the middle of Memphis. Explore its 126 acres on an Old Forest Nature Hike, second Saturdays and final Sundays monthly at 10 a.m., when Citizens to Preserve Overton Park guides tours. It's a different place every season, but guide Naomi Van Tol reminds that wildlife-viewing, particularly bird-watching, is productive in winter, when you're seeing only the bones of the forest. Stay warm by balancing on the giant trunks of fallen trees as you wait for the red zip of a cardinal through the forest's wintry gray and brown skeleton. Tours wind about a mile along the forest trails and average an hour depending on weather and group stamina/interest. No reservations or fees are required but donations to the park are always welcome.

The Old Forest is located inside Overton Park,
which is bounded by North Parkway, East Parkway,
Poplar Avenue, and McLean Boulevard;
facebook.com/overtonparkforever

BONUS:
5 MORE WAYS TO PLAY IN OVERTON PARK

1. The Bike Arch. See that sculpted rainbow of bikes (and wheelchairs, unicycles, penny farthings, etc.) at the East Parkway entrance to the park? It's a visual feast with 320 sets of wheels—and a pedestrian gateway that connects Overton Park to the Shelby Farms Greenline, page 58, via a protected path called the Hampline.

2. The Greensward. There's no better place to play on a sunny day than this wide-open greenspace shared by Frisbee-throwers, kite-flyers, dog-walkers, freeze-taggers, and blanket-sitters. Bring your own fun and join in.

3. The Memphis Zoo. One of the country's top-ranked zoos debuted a new exhibit in 2016: Zambezi River Hippo Camp, inhabited by hippos, Nile crocodiles, and okapis. For uncrowded viewing, visit on a Sunday morning. Anytime, save a few dollars, and the Greensward, by street-parking in the adjacent neighborhood. *2000 Prentiss Pl., 901-333-6500, memphiszoo.org*

4. Overton Bark. Large and small dogs can have their days in separate, fenced play areas outfitted with pet water fountains and benches for their humans.

5. Rainbow Lake Playground. A 2013 redo added a classic merry-go-round and a 30-foot-long rope bridge in the sky (or eight feet off the ground, depending on your imagination).

Overton Park is bounded by North Parkway, East Parkway,
Poplar Avenue, and McLean Boulevard,
overtonpark.org

ROUND THE BASES
WITH ROCKEY

Memphis Redbirds at AutoZone Park

AutoZone Park is home to the Memphis Redbirds, Triple-A affiliate of the St. Louis Cardinals. Though it opened in 2000, the ballpark feels brand new thanks to a 2015 spruce-up. Still, you'll find me in the cheap seats: the lawn-seating areas behind left and right field known as the bluffs. Here, my daughter can dribble her ice cream (served in a miniature batting helmet, natch) and watch fireworks explode over downtown Memphis following Saturday home games. Following Sunday home games, kids can run the bases and take photos with Rockey, the Redbirds' mascot.

200 Union Ave., 901-721-6000,
memphisredbirds.com

JOIN
THE REVOLUTION

Revolutions Bicycle Cooperative

You'll find Revolutions through its own miniature bike arch at First Congregational Church. It's a hub for bike repair, instruction, and community—particularly in summer, when everyone's invited to Bike to Dinner with director Sylvia Crum and her family. These group rides are typically planned for Wednesday evenings to a different Midtown restaurant each excursion. Like Memphis's lineup of locally owned eateries, the crowd of riders who Bike to Dinner is growing all the time, Crum reports.

Whether you want to Bike to Dinner or explore on your own, check Spinlister.com to rent a city bike equipped with a basket or a family cargo bike from Revolutions's fleet.

1000 S. Cooper St., 901-726-6409,
revolutionsmemphis.wordpress.com
Hours vary

TRUMP
CENTRAL PARK

Shelby Farms Park

At 4,500 acres, Memphis's Shelby Farms Park is five times larger than New York City's Central Park. In other words, it *can* be all things to all people, especially when its two-year renovation project, Heart of the Park, wraps in 2016.

Even before Heart of the Park, Shelby Farms tracked steady improvement. Its destination play space, the Woodland Discovery Playground, opened in 2011, daring kids to shoot down a 26-foot slide, spider-crawl across a web of ropes, and dangle from a teeter-totter swing. In 2015, the Go Ape Treetop Adventure Course blended right into the park's pine forest, thrilling adventurers with sky-high zip lines across Pine Lake.

Go for these. Go for all of your old favorites—fishing, horseback riding, observing the resident herd of buffalo. And go for Heart of the Park, which will add, among other elements, walking and bike paths, a water play area, a new visitor center, and a restaurant and café designed by real-food champion Kimbal Musk.

500 N. Pine Lake Dr., 901-767-7275,
shelbyfarmspark.org

LOG 26.2
(OR SCREAM LIKE A, WELL, CHEERLEADER)

St. Jude Memphis Marathon Weekend

The St. Jude Memphis Marathon Weekend owns the first weekend in December annually. As long as you aren't crowd-averse, it's one of the best times to be in Memphis, when the spirit of the city is riding high on a sea of 20,000 people participating in the weekend's marathon, half-marathon, marathon relay, 5K, kids' marathon, and family fun run—and raising $8 million in the process. Registration opens in May. Backup plan: Make posters and gather cowbells Friday night before the race; station yourself Saturday along the marathon route to cheer. If you've been training, the marathon course reads like a "best of" Memphis as it tracks through downtown, Overton Park, page 68, and the St. Jude campus, page 135, where runners are cheered on by patients and their parents. (It's okay to get choked up at this point.) The race celebrates its 15th anniversary in 2016.

stjudemarathon.org

BRING YOUR BOARD
WITH YOU

Tobey Skate Park

If you need a glossary to decode what you're about to read, Tobey Park probably isn't for you. Then again, maybe it is, particularly if you're traveling with a skateboarder who needs a fix away from home. The park materialized in 2011 with banks, bowls, half-pipes, ledges, rails, and a snake run; in spring 2015, it added free learn-to-skate clinics and what's now called the Midsouth Triple Crown skateboarding competition. Follow the Skatelife Memphis calendar to catch these events and others.

> **Note:** Tobey Skate Park welcomes beginner to advanced skaters. Helmets and protective pads are required for skaters ages 12 and under.

2599 Avery Ave.,
skatelifememphis.org

STRETCH
FOR YOUR HOPS

Bendy Brewski Yoga Memphis

Bendy Brewski shifts yoga from the studio to a place that serves, maybe even makes, beer. It's a concept created by a Memphian who left the city, but who cared enough to share her idea back home. Show up to a class with or without experience, with or without a yoga mat, wearing a t-shirt and sweats if that's your thing. This is not get-gussied-up-and-bend-yourself-into-a-pretzel-to-pose-for-Instagram yoga. This is everyperson's yoga, with an instructor who might swear and tell jokes while you're practicing, who'll assist you into (or out of) a pose if you need it, who'll encourage you to get a good stretch and a little flow going in just 45 minutes. Because she, like you, is ultimately in it for the beer. Your $15 class fee includes a beer token.

At the time of publication, Bendy Brewski offers evening classes at High Cotton Brewing Co., page 95, and the Rec Room. (Rec Room is an all-ages play space, at least until 6 p.m., that's tricked out like your cool-friend-from-high-school's basement—if your friend had hot pizza on demand and a full bar in addition to video, table, and board games.)

P.S. If you're looking for yoga in all the unconventional places, you should know about these classes, too: Wednesdays at 6:15 a.m., Sunrise Yoga wakes up the Hughes Pavilion of the Dixon Gallery & Gardens, page 38, with a view to the Dixon's lush lawn. I'm more likely to roll into the 1 p.m. class on Thursdays at the Memphis Brooks Museum of Art, page 34, when yoga unfolds amid Baroque masterpieces and a classical guitarist might provide music.

Bendy Brewski Yoga Memphis
facebook.com/bendybrewskiyogamemphis

The Rec Room
3000 Broad Ave., 901-209-1137,
recroommemphis.com

Jan's Famous Toffee Bars at Muddy's Grind House, page 93. Photo credit: Amanda Raney.

FOOD AND DRINK

For this section that requires little introduction, I'll just make a note on organization: The following entries are ordered loosely around the occasions of breakfast, lunch, dinner, dessert, drinks, and detox. For my vegan readers, please get yourself to vegancrunk.blogspot.com, where Bianca Phillips, author of *Cookin' Crunk: Eatin' Vegan in the Dirty South,* shares her favorite places to eat vegan in the city (look for the Memphis Vegan Dining Guide link from her homepage).

We'll wrap by shopping for, and picking our own, foodie souvenirs.

START YOUR DAY
THE MEMPHIS WAY

Breakfast spots for any occasion

Chances are, you haven't had your coffee yet, so I'll make this easy:

You want a greasy-spoon with a story. The Arcade has been serving Memphis since 1919. If it's your first visit, request the Elvis booth and make movie connections aided by the historic marker outside. *540 S. Main St., 901-526-5757, arcaderestaurant.com*

You want an impeccable, but unpretentious, Sunday brunch. At Bounty on Broad, Chef Jackson Kramer mixes dinner-menu favorites with morning-time delicacies (maybe scallops with butternut squash, jowl bacon, and pecans). Reservations recommended. *2519 Broad Ave., 901-410-8131, bountyonbroad.com; credit card only*

You want to drive through. Because Rock'n Dough Pizza Co.'s Jeremy Denno uses his extra dough to make beignets. Because he crafts breakfast-sandwich gold using scratch-made bread and duck eggs from local farms. Because you can drive through (or dine in) for any or all of it. *3445 Poplar Ave., #1, 901-512-6760, rockndoughpizza.com*

You want to grab and go. Hit the kitchenette inside Toarmina Grocery & Deli, owned by the Toarmina family since 1949. The biscuits, scratch-made each morning, are soft and golden with a nice saltiness and visible pockets of butter throughout. *1486 Chelsea Ave., 901-278-3361; closed Sunday*

'CUE UP
SOME GRUB

My top three barbecue spots

For a food that brings people together, barbecue can be downright polarizing—especially in a 'cue capital like Memphis, where we're spoiled from our shoulders to our butts, and hotly opinionated. But I'm writing this book, so I'm laying out my top three. Let the debates commence.

Central BBQ. Hit the downtown location where more tables = less (or no) wait. I'm still pulling for the pulled pork nachos. Drizzle your basket with Central's molasses-based sauce to achieve the ultimate salty/spicy/sweet trifecta. *147 E. Butler Ave., 901-672-7760, cbqmemphis.com*

Cozy Corner. Cozy Corner is so beloved, Memphians raised money to help the restaurant recover from a 2015 fire. Though reconstruction was still rolling at publication time, nothing can quash the goodness of a Cozy Corner sliced pork sandwich, stacked with slaw on a sesame seed roll and sauced hot for a slow burn. If you don't see anyone at the original location (745 N. Parkway), head across the street to 726, where the crew's been keeping shop inside Encore Café. *901-527-9158, cozycornerbbq.com; closed Sunday and Monday*

Elwood's Shack. Elwood's menu covers just about every base, from pizza to a glorious trout taco. You may walk in with the best intentions to try these things. You will smell pork, wings, brisket, and ribs smoldering in the smoker built into the side of Elwood's unassuming building. You will order the barbecue. *4523 Summer Ave., 901-761-9898, elwoodsshack.com*

SNIFF OUT
THE WORLD CHAMPIONSHIP
BARBECUE COOKING CONTEST

Memphis in May's World Championship Barbecue Cooking Contest
The World Championship Barbecue Cooking Contest (WCBCC) draws around 250 teams competing in categories like whole hog and ribs. Then thousands of people smell it cooking and follow. So mark your calendar for the second weekend in May. Just don't be the one who shows up ignorant of the cardinal rule: Teams may not serve the general public (health regulations). Still, there are ways to savor the experience:

- Join the Cooker's Caravan, free tours guided by competitors, Thursday and Friday of the WCBCC.

- Register in advance for the Kingsford Tour of Champions. For $12, you'll taste samples prepared by select teams; then vote for your favorite.

- To build a relationship with a team, target daytime Thursday or Friday of the contest. Ask a competitor about his or her cooker (most of them like to show off) and see where the conversation goes.

- For a visual feast, wander. Teams construct booths where they live and work throughout the contest, booths that might be one or three stories high and incorporate tiki bars or animatronic dinosaurs. General admission to the WCBCC, usually $10 and free 11 a.m.–1 p.m. Thursday and Friday of the contest, buys you all the gawking you want.

> The WCBCC takes place in Tom Lee Park along Riverside Drive in downtown Memphis. memphisinmay.org/worldchampionshipbbqcontest

FEED
YOUR SOUL

Soul food favorites

Soul food can be many things. There's the meat-and-three (meat choice + 2 side items + 1 bread choice); fried chicken and wings you'll order in multiples; buffets that lay out all of your choices, from catfish and pork chops to lima beans and yams. But there is just one thing that describes all soul food restaurants. As Kaia Brewer puts it, "It's someone really putting the love to what they're doing."

Brewer is chef and owner at Lunchbox Eats, where she's created a family-friendly space with board games and a retro schoolhouse feel. She classifies her menu as "soul fusion." You'll understand when you taste Brewer's reimagining of classic meatloaf as a burger crowned with creamy mashed potatoes, tomato gravy, and crispy onions.

Now that you've met the next generation of Memphis soul food, meet its pioneers. And don't be surprised when they show you some love.

Alcenia's. Owner B.J. Chester-Tamayo stays busy running to and from her kitchen retrieving made-to-order meals, but she's never too busy to hug her guests. Go on a Saturday morning for chicken and waffles. B.J.'s fried chicken is photoshoot-ready, its exterior nicely textured and browned. Inside, it's savory and juicy, a waffle's best friend. For its part, the waffle is crusty in all the right places with cinnamon hiding in its squares.

The Four Way. Yes, this restaurant has helped anchor Memphis's Soulsville neighborhood since 1946. Yes, it's the one that's hosted Martin Luther King Jr., Drake, and everyone in between. All of these things aside, you should eat here because owner Willie Earl Bates, and his English peas, are so sweet, you won't need dessert. (The man once gave me heartfelt counsel when a lunch date stood me up.) The peas are just one choice on a list of a dozen or so vegetables at this meat-and-three, which reminds me: If the inclusion of macaroni and cheese or dressing on a list of vegetables strikes you as odd, well, bless your heart.

Alcenia's
317 N. Main St.,
901-523-0200,
alcenias.com
Closed Sunday and Monday

The Four Way
998 Mississippi Blvd.,
901-507-1519,
fourwaymemphis.com
Closed Monday

Lunchbox Eats
288 S. 4th St.,
901-526-0820
Closed Sunday

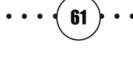
FRY
MORE CHICKEN

Uncle Lou's Fried Chicken

Uncle Lou's is filed into a strip mall, but there's nothing ordinary about it. Like Alcenia's fried chicken on the previous page, Uncle Lou's is cooked to order. But the exterior is thin, exposing the juiciest meat I've found in town.

Be ready with your order when you approach the counter. Specify how many pieces you want, white or dark, and which variety: homestyle, sweet spicy love mild, or sweet spicy love hot. If it's your first time, go with at least a three-piece to sample them all. The latter will leave you licking your fingers, momentarily red from the family-recipe sauce, which is addictively sweet, spicy, and cinnamon-y.

Whether you grab a table or take your chicken to go, pay attention: Orders come up surprisingly fast here, but the cashier may still call you "baby."

3633 Millbranch Rd.,
901-332-2367,
unclelousfriedchicken.com

FEAST
ON FARM-TO-TABLE

Farm-to-table favorites

These aren't the only Memphis restaurants that emphasize local, seasonal food and support area farmers. They *are* my top picks.

The Farmer. Restaurateur Mac Edwards supports local producers so thoroughly, it's possible you'll rub elbows with him while shopping the Memphis Farmers Market, page 101. No surprise, then, that The Farmer's menu features pan-seared Mississippi catfish and sides like braised greens, so exquisitely flavored, I won't even give them my usual dousing of pepper vinegar. *262 S. Highland St., 901-324-2221, thefarmermemphis.com*

Rizzo's Diner. Year-round, Chef Michael Patrick keeps a vegetable plate on his menu. It's always different, but always inventive, for what Chef Patrick sees in a farmer's offering is different from what I see. He has a way of combining flavors and coaxing flavors out of fruits and vegetables that I never knew was possible. *492 S. Main St., 901-304-6985, rizzosmemphis.com*

Trolley Stop Market. I love Trolley Stop Market for its family-friendliness and food you can feel good about. From the burgers to the pizza—scratch-made dough layered with grilled meats and a bounty of veggies—the menu honors local farmers and producers, including owners Keith and Jill Forrester. Shop the restaurant's local-makers market while you wait. *704 Madison Ave., 901-526-1361, trolleystopmarket.com; closed Sunday*

EAT THIS BURGER
OUTSIDE

Shelby Forest General Store

Count on Shelby Forest General Store for taxidermy décor and the essentials: beer, disc golf supplies, and short-order standards so messy they beg to be eaten outside. Lucky you: The store's front porch lines up picnic tables for lunching and people-watching, particularly the yin-yang of motorcyclists and road bikers heading for the shady hills of neighboring Meeman-Shelby Forest State Park, page 63. If you're unsure what to order, the cheeseburger all the way—with a wad of napkins—is solid. Place your order at the counter, select a drink from one of the coolers, and take your seat on the porch. The staff will bring you your burger, wrapped in wax paper, the second it comes off the griddle.

Bonus: When the weather's kind, usually March through May and again just after Labor Day through November, the front porch hosts live music, too. Listen for bluegrass jams, acoustic bits, and the like Saturday, noon–3 p.m.; Sunday, 12:30–3:30 p.m.

7729 Benjestown Rd., Millington,
901-876-5770,
shelbyforestgeneralstore.com

BONUS:
4 MORE DIVES WITH DELICIOUS BURGERS

1. Earnestine & Hazel's. Order the Soul Burger not because it's the only thing on the menu, but because it's beautifully simple. This burger is not big enough to eat you; it's not dressed to excess or to impress via hoity-toity toppings. It's just a standard-sized bun, thin patty, onions, cheese, pickle, and tangy "Soul Sauce." *531 S. Main St., 901-523-9754, earnestineandhazelsjukejoint.com*

2. Huey's. Huey's serves patties as simple or as decked out as you like (the Bluff City, for example, piles on smoked cheddar, bacon, onion straws, and barbecue sauce). To get the best feel for the restaurant's place in Memphis history, visit the Midtown location, and attempt to shoot a toothpick into the ceiling like those who've gone before you. Hint: Use your straw. *1927 Madison Ave., 901-726-4372, hueyburger.com*

3. Jerry's Sno Cones. At this Memphis dessert icon, page 92, hamburger patties are ground fresh daily, hand-formed, and studded with just the right amount of "bark" from the business of griddling. I favor loaded versions like the Blue Mushroom, layered with tangy blue cheese spread, mushrooms, and onions. *1657 Wells Station Rd., 901-767-2659; closed Sunday; cash only*

4. The P & H Café. Inside this smoky cocoon, just in time for dinner, something delicious happens. Beef patties get stuffed with flavor-packed combinations, say, Swiss and mushrooms or cheddar and jalapenos. Choose from the handful of beers on tap and prepare for oozy goodness. *1532 Madison Ave., 901-726-0906, pandhcafe.com; closed Sunday*

EAT
AROUND THE WORLD

Globally inspired favorites

You can find globally inspired restaurants throughout Memphis, but the following streets stack them up like shawarma on a spit:

Madison Avenue. I start at Madison's downtown end, anchored by The Brass Door, Memphian Seamus Loftus's ode to the public houses of his native Ireland. Duck inside the pub's gorgeous century-old building for house favorites like beer-battered fish with house-cut chips. Progressing east, I break at Casablanca Restaurant, an ambrosia of Middle Eastern spices and ingredients. Start with the iced tea brewed with fresh mint, ginger root, pure honey, and sage, and put Southern sweet tea on notice. Continue east on Madison to Overton Square, page 44, for German, Indian, Japanese, and Mexican options.

South Cooper Street. This is where global inspiration goes upscale. At Bari Ristorante e Enoteca, design the cheese plate of your dreams and flow through courses of pasta and rustic fish dishes. That's the Southern Italian way, as Chef Jason Severs's grandmother taught him. From Bari, head south on Cooper Street to the Cooper-Young neighborhood and Tsunami, where small plates evidence Chef Ben Smith's culinary training in the Pacific Rim. He changes the plates nightly, so you could be in for sea bass with pineapple stir fry, wagyu with wasabi butter, or something else altogether. Reservations recommended for both restaurants.

Summer Avenue. When it comes to food, Summer Avenue has the whole world in its hands. I go for authentic Mexican, starting at Tacos Los Jarochos. As good things do, these tacos come in threes. Choose which meat will crown your corn tortillas (I like the steak) and go "all the way" for a topping salad of fresh cilantro, lime wedges, simmered and raw onion, and tomato. Dressing your order with the truck's tomatillo salsa will set your world on fire. Extinguish it just down the road with La Michoacana's homemade frozen treats: ice cream, puckery chamoyadas, and paletas studded with fruit that are (almost) too pretty to eat.

Bari Ristorante e Enoteca
22 S. Cooper St.,
901-722-2244,
barimemphis.com

The Brass Door
152 Madison Ave.,
901-572-1813,
thebrassdoor.com

Casablanca Restaurant
1707 Madison Ave.,
901-421-6949,
casablancamemphis.com

La Michoacana
4091 Summer Ave.,
901-590-1901

Tacos Los Jarochos
4900 Summer Ave.,
901-314-5735
Cash only

Tsunami
928 S. Cooper St.,
901-274-2556,
tsunamimemphis.com
Closed Sunday

SEE WHAT THE BUZZ IS ABOUT
ON A BUDGET

Celeb chef favorites

In Memphis, we put our dives—the solid ones—up there with the nicest restaurants in town. We like good food, and we like it to be approachable. Maybe that's why some of our most accomplished chefs have opened casual outposts and started surprising traditions (I'm looking at you, 25-cent martini). Want to check out a few of the chefs who class up Memphis's culinary landscape—without the white-tablecloth prices? Try my top three:

Felicia Suzanne's. Chef Felicia Suzanne Willett serves dinner with one exception: Friday lunch. Do as I do and invite a few friends to share starters and sides: deviled eggs spiked with hot sauce, delicately fried green tomatoes, meaty gumbo . . . all of which, incidentally, pair well with the 25-cent martinis Willett offers exclusively at this seating. *80 Monroe Ave. L1, 901-523-0877, feliciasuzanne.com; closed Sunday and Monday*

Porcellino's Craft Butcher. Chefs Andy Ticer and Michael Hudman created this foodie heaven, at once a butcher shop, sundry store, coffee and tea bar, and restaurant. I go at lunch for the Hudbano sandwich with an order of sweet potato fries, both large enough to share. The Hudbano is the best interpretation of a Cuban sandwich I've found in town, layered with mojo pork and pickles on scratch-made bolillo bread. The otherworldly fries are cozied up with bites of charred Vidalia onion beneath a melt of poblano-spiced cheese. *711 W. Brookhaven Cir., 901-762-6656, porcellinoscraftbutcher.com*

The Second Line. The Second Line exposes the grit on Kelly English's chef whites, accumulated over years of surviving odd kitchen jobs on cold leftovers. Compound that with English's Louisiana heritage, and you get a menu full of honest, sustaining foods like the Johnny Snack, a po'boy of hot ham and cheese with gravy. Patio seating's a must in good weather. *2144 Monroe Ave., 901-590-2829, secondlinememphis.com*

MAKE IT
A SUPREME

Jerry's Sno Cones

What is a Jerry's Sno Cone?

It's no craggy ball of ice in a sad paper cone. It's not so smooth it could pass for ice cream. Yet it's dense enough to warrant a Styrofoam cup and plastic spoon, and versatile enough to take on some 70 flavor combinations. It starts with ice soft-packed like snow. Flavored syrups are added; owner David Acklin makes them all by hand. And if you make yours a supreme, it gets a core of soft-serve ice cream, which melts into the ice for a sweet, milky chill.

Flavors range from the straightforward—Almond Joy tastes just like the candy bar and even better with a tunnel of chocolate soft serve—to the needs-translation: Tiger's Blood, a local favorite, blends strawberry with coconut.

There are a few places so beloved in Memphis that queuing up with the locals outside of said places becomes part of the experience. Jerry's is one of them. So chat with the folks lined up around you. No doubt you'll meet someone who's been coming here since Jerry's opened in the 1970s. The sun may be blazing; you may be standing in a parking lot. But this is Memphis in all of its sweet, gritty glory— congratulations for seeking it out.

1657 Wells Station Rd.,
901-767-2659
Closed Sunday; cash only

BONUS:
5 MORE WINS FOR YOUR SWEET TOOTH

1. A&R Bar-B-Que. The extended Pollard family makes fried pies daily: perfectly browned half-moons sprinkled with sugar and filled with apple, peach, or sweet potato. They're so good, you'll say you're going to share, but you won't. *1802 Elvis Presley Blvd., 901-774-7444, aandrbbq.com*

2. Makeda's. Biting into Makeda's sandy little butter cookies activates the recipe's butter, turning each morsel to salty-sweet velvet in your mouth. Find the largest variety at the Airways location. *2370 Airways Blvd., 901-745-2667, makedascookies.com; closed Sunday*

3. Muddy's. Memphis's beloved from-scratch bakery opened that second location I promised you in Edition 1 of this book, dubbed Muddy's Grind House for its full-blown coffee bar. Do as Muddy's creator Kat Gordon does and pair a slice of Nancy's Boy coconut chess pie with a fresh cup. *585 S. Cooper St., 901-443-4144, muddysbakeshop.com; closed Sunday*

4. The Peabody Memphis. Nightly, a dessert cart rolls into the hotel lobby that will make you stagger. Each selection, created by The Peabody Memphis pastry team, resembles a tiny present tempting you to unwrap it, like the tiramisu cradled in a chocolate cup. *149 Union Ave., 901-529-4000, peabodymemphis.com*

5. Westy's. Jake's Hot Fudge Pie is more slab than slice, more fudge than brownie, all made-in-house goodness. Enjoy yours warm, topped with vanilla ice cream, chocolate sauce, and whipped cream. *346 N. Main St., 901-543-8646, westysmemphis.com*

DRINK THE WATER
(IT'S WHAT MAKES THE BEER TASTE SO GOOD.)

Memphis craft beer

Beneath Beale and Elvis Presley Boulevard and all those other Memphis streets you're beating, four natural aquifers flow with pure water. Beer is 95 percent water. How good is beer brewed in Memphis? *So* good.

You know what's crazy, though? Edition 1 of this book snapshotted Memphis's craft brew movement, with the exception of 1990s pioneer Boscos Squared, in its early stages. Two years later, it's nice to report that what was trending is playing for keeps, adding tap rooms and programming and raising awareness of what good beer can be.

Sample the following Memphis craft brews at bars, restaurants, and growler-filling stations around town, or go directly to the breweries, as available:

Boscos Squared. At this outpost of Tennessee's first brew pub, you'll find several selections brewed on-site and on tap—order the sampler for an overview. You should also taste what Ghost River's brewing (that's the side project of Boscos's owners that grew into its own outfit, with its own recipes, in 2008). For years, Ghost River's been selling growlers off its dock, but in 2016 the brewery plans to reinstate tours and open a tap room. *Boscos Squared, 2120 Madison Ave., 901-432-2222, boscosbeer.com. Ghost River Brewing, 827 S. Main St., 901-278-0140, ghostriverbrewing.com; closed Sunday*

High Cotton Brewing Co. Since Edition 1 of this book, High Cotton found a home by beautifully repurposing a warehouse in downtown's Edge District. Among the beers in the tap room, you're sure to find the ESB: copper-colored, malty-sweet, and (super) drinkable. Sit inside or out, play a board or card game, and take the Saturday afternoon brewer's tour. *598 Monroe Ave., 901-543-4444, highcottonbrewing. com; closed Monday–Wednesday*

Memphis Made Brewing Co. Memphis Made found its home in a warehouse in the Cooper-Young neighborhood. Its taps pour seasonal and limited releases plus the flagship Lucid Kolsch, a pale German ale. Play cornhole in the cavernous space; when you're hungry, check for a food truck or order from Aldo's Pizza Pies next door—they deliver direct to the brewery. Tours Saturday and Sunday. *768 S. Cooper St., 901-207-5343, memphismadebrewing.com; closed Monday–Thursday*

Wiseacre Brewing Co. Memphis's first tap room was around for Edition 1 of this book, but it's progressed. You can now enjoy your beer on expanded decks outside, attend beer-education events and May's Taste the Rarity Beer Festival, and take a tour most days the brewery's open. Tap room selections always include Tiny Bomb, Wiseacre's award-winning American Pilsner sweetened with local wildflower honey. *2783 Broad Ave., wiseacrebrew.com; closed Sunday–Tuesday; credit card only*

TOAST TO
THE MUSIC

Delta Blues Winery and Old Millington Winery

West Tennessee is no wine country. But the wineries of our region have their own ambience, a trifecta of friendly winemakers, small-batch crafting, and pretty, rural settings that double as live music venues.

At Old Millington Winery, Perry Welch skews the profile sweet for Southern tastes. Breeze by for a tasting, or do as I do and wait for a Sunday afternoon when Welch hosts live music outside the winery, April through June and again in September and October. For a nominal cover, you can enter with a cooler or picnic basket, blankets and chairs, even your own beer, and buy wine by the bottle on-site. I think the Delta Blush pairs beautifully with a sunny afternoon and stripped-down blues by Dr. David Evans.

At Delta Blues Winery, Jim Wilson and friends use West Tennessee grapes to make several styles of wine, though the Veranda Peach sells best—add a splash of sparkling wine and a few peach slices, and you've got yourself a Blues Bellini. Jim's team offers tastings and tours, but Friday nights are the main event, when local bands play and you can bring a picnic and purchase wine by the glass or bottle. Ask about Sunday singer/songwriter nights when you're on-site.

Delta Blues Winery
6585 Stewart Rd., Lakeland,
901-829-4685,
deltablueswinery.com
Closed Monday

Old Millington Winery
6748 Old Millington Rd., Millington,
901-873-4114,
oldmillingtonwinery.com
Closed Monday and Tuesday

West Tennessee Wine Trail
winetrailofwestttn.com

GET SPIRITED

Pyramid Vodka

For some time now, I've been able to buy Pyramid Vodka at my local liquor store (thanks, Joe's). But as I was researching for this edition, something momentous happened: Pyramid opened for tours and tastings, the first craft distiller to do so in Memphis. Stop by Wednesday through Friday, 2–5 p.m., or Saturday, 10 a.m.–2 p.m. Even if the place looks quiet, ring the bell outside and someone will welcome you in.

Ian Thomas, Pyramid's director of production, toured me around. His vibe was part science teacher, part proud papa as he showed me every step of his process.

If the science goes over your head, focus on this: Remember how good I told you Memphis water is (page 94)? Imagine what happens when it's used to proof spirits. Thomas and team start with corn farmed locally, milling it on-site along with malted barley. They cook the corn in that Memphis aquifer water, then ferment, distill, filter, and bottle the spirit on-site. At the end of your tour, they'll pour it for you, too.

And that's how Memphis does grain-to-glass. Check out the rainbow of medals decorating Pyramid's lobby, slated to become a tasting room.

802 Royal Ave.,
901-576-8844,
pyramidvodka.com
Closed Sunday–Tuesday

DETOX

Healthy favorites

In the course of researching for this edition, I've consumed doughnuts for dinner, fried pies for lunch, and shots of barbecue sauce at breakfast. When it's time to detox, I check into . . .

LYFE Kitchen. Order at the counter like you would at a fast-casual joint. The food comes fast, but it isn't "fast food," or completely casual, for that matter: LYFE puts serious thought into its ingredients and preparations. Calorie and sodium counts are watched. Nothing is fried. Yet this food tastes good, whether you order the grass-fed beef burger or the vegan Thai Red Curry Bowl, my go-to that's fragrant with garlic and lime. Wine, beer, and a menu for kids, too, all from a chain now headquartered, and growing, in Memphis. *6201 Poplar Ave., 901-684-5333, and 272 S. Main St., 901-526-0254; lyfekitchen.com*

Raw Girls. Two food trucks are the vehicles for Amy and Hannah Pickle's good-for-you offerings. Menus change weekly and sway with the seasons, so you might find white bean soup, avocado toast with blistered tomatoes, or a raw taco salad of fresh pico de gallo, homemade guac, and spicy walnut meat over organic local greens. Any time of year, I brake for a cold-pressed Merry Fabulous, a jewel-toned elixir of beets, pineapple, lemon, ginger, and basil. *242 Cooper St. (in the Eclectic Eye parking lot), closed Monday and Tuesday, and 5502 Poplar Ave. (in the Hollywood Feed parking lot), closed Sunday–Tuesday; facebook.com/rawgirlsmemphis*

PICK
YOUR OWN

Jones Orchard

In season, I can buy my peaches from Jones Orchard at local markets like those on the opposite page. But at least once a year, I pick my own. Sure, it saves a few dollars, but I like driving all rumbly-tumbly along the gravel roads into the orchard off of Big Creek Church Road, where the peaches blaze like fireballs in the trees and beg to be eaten right there, juice dribbling onto the grass. Jones operates three pick-your-own orchards in Memphis and neighboring Millington and publishes a handy ripening calendar online so you'll know when to go for peaches or strawberries or nectarines or plums or apples or what have you.

6824 Big Creek Church Rd., Millington,
901-872-0703,
jonesorchard.com

BONUS:
5 MORE SPOTS TO BAG FOODIE SOUVENIRS

I'm not dissuading you from buying the Elvis sunglasses. I'm just saying that food makes an authentic, satisfying souvenir, and these markets deliver:

1. Bobby Lanier Farm Park Market. Food trucks and a small farmers market set amid a community garden and yard with stick ponies for the kids. *Behind Germantown Elementary School, 2730 Cross Country Dr., Germantown, germantown-tn.gov; Thursday afternoons, June through August*

2. Curb Market. Shop this mini-market for Aunt Lizzie's cheese straws, Wolf River popcorn, and a spoil of barbecue sauces. *596 S. Cooper St., 901-453-6880, curbmarket901.com*

3. Memphis Botanic Garden Farmers Market. Amid beautiful Memphis Botanic Garden, page 66, shop and treat yourself to an all-natural Mama D's popsicle. *750 Cherry Rd., 901-636-4100, memphisbotanicgarden.com; Wednesday afternoons, April through October*

4. Memphis Farmers Market. More than 75 vendors, food trucks, and weekly programming from live music to cooking demos make this market an affair. *G.E. Patterson Avenue and South Front Street, memphisfarmersmarket.org; Saturdays, April through late November*

5. Miss Cordelia's Grocery. Shelves spotlight locally made artisanal foods (mmm . . . Shotwell Candy Co. caramels). *737 Harbor Bend Rd., 901-526-4772, misscordelias.com*

Hope Clayburn's Soul Scrimmage, page 131.
Photo credit: Brian Anderson.

MUSIC AND NIGHTLIFE

When *USA Today* released its 10BEST list of global music attractions in 2015, Memphis came in three times . . . in the top five. I don't have to explain to you why music is significant in Memphis, but I do hope you'll hear more than the echoes of our legends around town. In this section, then, we'll talk landmarks, but we'll also take insider tours and listen for voices that amplify Memphis's living, breathing, resounding music tradition at unique venues and festivals.

Two more things:
I ordered these experiences loosely from day to night.
For an aggregate of live music listings, consult the *Memphis Flyer,* free in stands citywide and at memphisflyer.com.

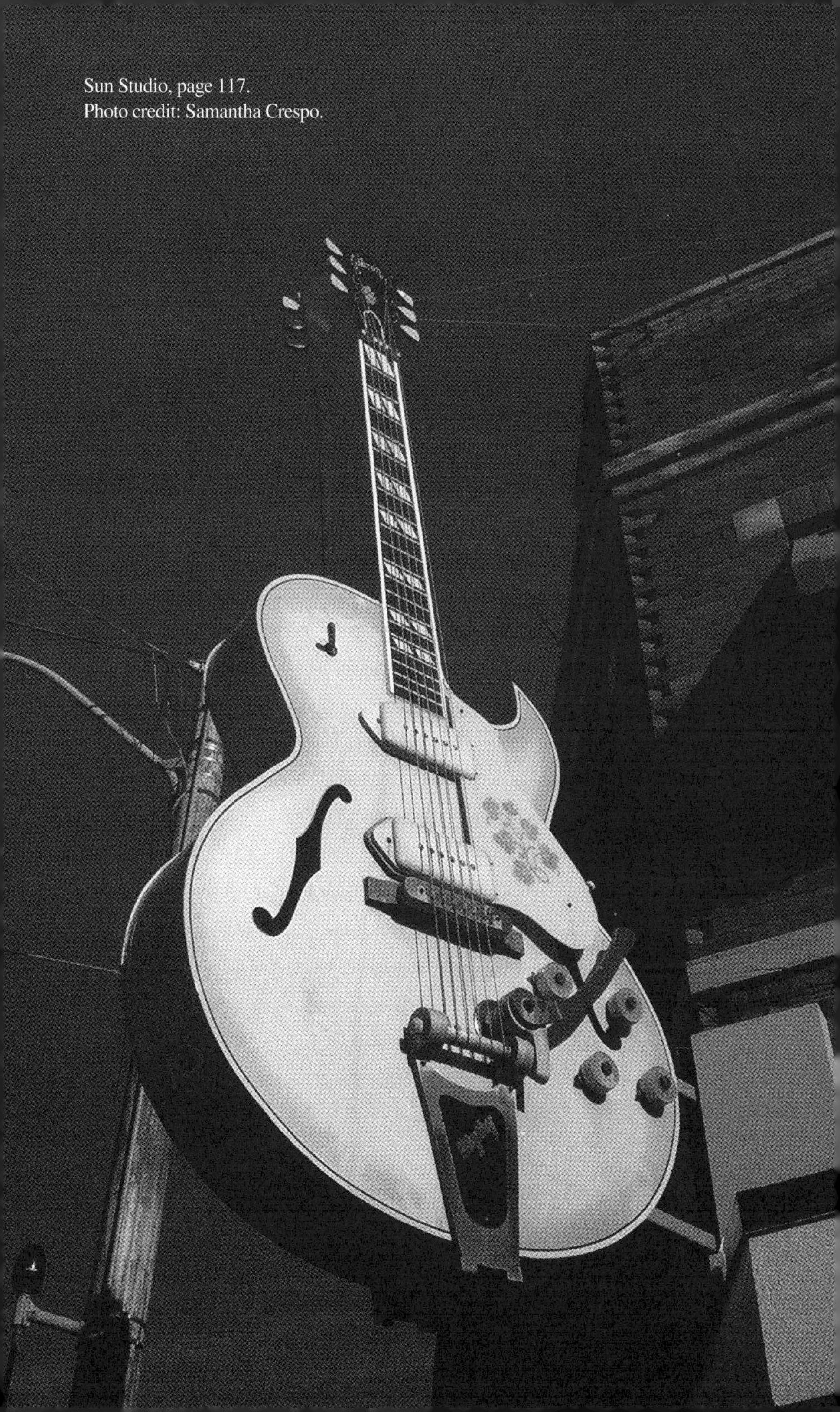

Sun Studio, page 117.
Photo credit: Samantha Crespo.

SPEND SUNDAY MORNING
WITH REVEREND AL

Al Green's Full Gospel Tabernacle

If you're looking for the Al Green who made music history at Memphis's Royal Studios in the 1970s, pick up the compilation from Shangri-La, page 115. If you're looking to meet Al where he is today, get to his Full Gospel Tabernacle on a Sunday morning. Arrive at 11:30 a.m., despite what you might read on TripAdvisor, unless you want to be called out by the Reverend himself. And you better be committed, because you probably won't leave until at least 2 p.m.

That might sound like a slog. It isn't. By 11:30, congregants are already taking turns at the mic and the small choir and seven-piece band are settling in. They set into motion a flow of spoken word and song that surges when Reverend Al joins. When his stream of conversation, testimony, social commentary, and prayer ripples into music, worshippers pull out tambourines and dance in the aisles. Choir singers fan themselves even in the dead of winter. The Reverend pauses at times to play air guitar. You will, at least, clap your hands; it's impossible not to feel joy in these moments.

The flow only slows for the offering, when envelopes go 'round and everyone's invited, row by row, to drop something in the plate in front of Reverend Al. From here, he delivers a short sermon much like his initial address and sends you out on a song.

787 Hale Rd.

BRUNCH WITH
"THE WALKING JUKEBOX"

Joyce Cobb at Boscos Squared

Joyce Cobb moved to Memphis in the 1970s when Jim Stewart signed her to a country-western recording contract with Volt, a subsidiary of Stax Records, page 116, right before the studio closed. We're glad she stayed. Though her influence echoes all around—hear her spinning world music on WEVL FM 89.9 or teaching jazz vocals at the University of Memphis— Cobb's notes go down smooth with Sunday brunch at Boscos Squared (11:30 a.m.–2:30 p.m.). For 16 years, she's been singing from the book of American pop standards at the restaurant, now with a multipiece band that might include fiddle, saxophone, and flute. For its part, Boscos's brunch menu performs variations on the Bloody Mary, Bellini, and mimosa.

2120 Madison Ave.,
901-432-2222,
boscosbeer.com

JOIN THE CARAVAN

Beale Street Caravan

Here's one you can do from anywhere in the world: Tune into *Beale Street Caravan*, the weekly, hour-long radio broadcast of Memphis music and its "derivative forms" to three million-plus listeners across the globe. Define derivative? "If we can connect the dots to Memphis, that's a story we need to tell," explains *Caravan* executive producer Kevin Cubbins, and so the series swings from blues to folk to gospel to rock-and-roll to roots to soul and so on, as performed by music-makers based in Memphis and beyond. Cubbins's crew records at concerts and festivals across the U.S. to present two acts per broadcast, and weekly guest spots can be just as entertaining: Listen for personalities like Ardent Studios's producer/engineer Adam Hill, who might show up to chat about recording ZZ Top in Memphis, or anything else he's worked (or working) on.

You can always visit the *Caravan's* website to learn where and when to listen and to find archived broadcasts. But in 2015, the show ushered in extras to celebrate its 20th season on air, acquiring a mobile recording van and adopting a storefront—which feels more like a living room—for hosting periodic events. Subscribe to the *Caravan's* monthly newsletter for details, and anticipate a new annual event in spring: the Star-Lite Revue. In the spirit of musical revues produced through the 1960s and '70s by Memphis's WDIA, the nation's first radio station programmed by and for African Americans, the event will bring a patchwork of artists together for a sweet-sounding collaboration.

49 Union Ave.,
bealestreetcaravan.com

SEE WHAT'S NEW
ABOUT BEING BLUE

Blues Hall of Fame

Know what the best part of writing this book was? Taking you to the places I could only tease you with in Edition 1, like the Blues Hall of Fame. The Blues Foundation has actually been inducting individuals, recordings, and writings into a virtual hall since 1980. In May 2015, following a $2.5-million construction project and monumental artifact collection effort, that virtual hall materialized.

Go for changing exhibits in the lobby, a reading nook stocked with books composed by and about blues legends, and mini-galleries. Each of these vignettes is anchored by a large touch screen that illuminates a different set of performers through photographs, film clips, and music—a digital docent of sorts. Related artifacts, from Bobby "Blue" Bland's captain's hat to Lead Belly's bow tie, round out each vignette. Plan an hour or so to see it all.

421 S. Main St.,
901-527-2583,
blues.org

EXPERIENCE GRACELAND
ON ANY BUDGET

Graceland, plus Elvis Week freebies

Graceland is one of the most visited homes in the U.S. In other words, Elvis Presley Enterprises doesn't need my help convincing you to visit. Yet some of you are reading this insisting Graceland isn't for you. I hear you, and I raise you:

"Been there, done that." Yay for you. But know that exhibits in and around the mansion change regularly, so you might see something new, like the Graceland Archives Experience now tacked onto VIP and Platinum tickets.

"I'm not an Elvis fan." Maybe not, but I bet you like the Beatles or James Brown or Katy Perry, just a few of the artists who claim Elvis as an inspiration.

"I'm on a budget." While you're saving up for that Entourage VIP Tour, you can do loads for free or just a few bucks. "During Elvis Week [annually in mid-August], there's the official list of activities and the unofficial," Mike Freeman, owner of Memphis Road Tours, will tell you. For the energy of Elvis Week without giving up a hunk o' cash, check out these word-of-mouth to-dos:

- **King's Signature Hotel.** A tradeshow stuffs two ballrooms with memorabilia and records, plus free tribute performances. *1471 E. Brooks Rd., 901-332-3500*

- **Marlowe's Ribs & Restaurant.** Time drinks or dinner with one of the many free tribute shows that roll through the restaurant during Elvis

Week. "It's like getting Elvis Week for the cost of a beer," Freeman nudges. *4381 Elvis Presley Blvd., 901-332-4159, marlowesmemphis.com*

Note too that annually on the night of August 15, the gates of Graceland open for free to anyone wishing to participate in the Candlelight Vigil. The procession usually lasts into the morning of August 16, the anniversary of Elvis's death. Parking is free, too. And any time of year, taking a photo starring the Graceland gates costs nothing; nor does a tiptoe up the driveway to the Meditation Garden, available most days of the year, 7:30 to 8:30 a.m.

Graceland
3734 Elvis Presley Blvd.,
901-332-3322,
graceland.com
Closed select days in winter

Memphis Road Tours
901-289-7401,
memphisroadtours.com

TOUR
A GUITAR FACTORY

Gibson Beale Street Showcase and St. Blues Guitar Workshop
In the Gibson Guitar universe, only the Gibson Beale Street Showcase invites tours. Visitors ages 5 and up can move between stations designed for each phase of the production process, a mix of machine and handwork that culminates in persnickety final touches: the painting and testing of Gibson's ES line of guitars. You'll especially like this tour if spotting a guitar-in-progress for Dave Grohl or someone like him star-strikes you. Or if you're a guitarist, play a demo instrument in the retail center before or after your walkabout. Still, the most gratifying tours here glimpse working luthiers, so ask which days are best when you reserve.

Like its boutique approach to production, a tour of St. Blues Guitar Workshop is custom. Monday through Saturday by appointment, an exec or tech will show you the front and back of the operation. Don't be afraid to ask anything, whether to try a hand at fretting or playing one of the instruments. Allow extra time to hang at the "Whammy Bar" where Greg Mitchell crafts cigar box guitars, and to meet Tom "TK" Keckler, the father of the Bluesmaster who spends most afternoons checking instrument quality and relating his encounters with Jeff Beck and Led Zeppelin.

Gibson Beale Street Showcase,
145 Lt. George W. Lee Ave., 901-544-7998,
gibson.com

St. Blues Guitar Workshop,
645 Marshall Ave., 901-578-3588,
saintblues.com

FEEL
THE VIBRATION

Memphis Drum Shop

If nearly every musician coming through Memphis makes a pilgrimage to Memphis Drum Shop (MDS), why shouldn't you? Part retail store, part percussionist's shrine, MDS stocks souvenir sticks, hosts concerts and clinics on a soundstage, and provides an unamplified electronic kit you can demo. For an exclusive, register for Sonic Massage with Faye Henry, usually offered final Saturdays monthly at 1 p.m. ($60 for the hour). Inside MDS's private gong chamber, Henry plays 40 Paiste-brand gongs, sized from seven inches to seven feet in diameter, and arranged in a circle. The physical vibration in-the-round can be therapeutic, if not transformative. Contact the shop to register.

878 S. Cooper St., 901-276-2328,
memphisdrumshop.com
Closed Sunday

CONNECT THE DOTS

Memphis Music Hall of Fame and Memphis Rock 'n' Soul Museum
The Memphis Rock 'n' Soul Museum came on the scene in 2000, a Smithsonian affiliate that flaunts relics like Ike Turner's first piano and the original lyrics to "Heartbreak Hotel." Still, my favorite thing here is the audio tour included with admission: 100 tunes sing the story of Memphis music, cataloging influences like Sister Rosetta Tharpe and Robert Johnson. (You can hear, and almost see, the story play out on Beale Street when you take the museum's audio walking tour, page 4.)

In 2012, the Memphis Music Hall of Fame began inducting members; a physical Hall coalesced in 2015. It narrows the scope of the Rock 'n' Soul to inducted Hall of Famers, presenting a concentrated collection: You might find Three 6 Mafia's Oscar for Best Original Song near a Lansky Bros. suit Johnny Cash procured decades ago in this very building. Memorabilia is added with each new class of inductees.

As a new museum, the Hall of Fame emphasizes interactivity. Scour touch-screen archives and play games like "Finish the Influences," a six-degrees-of-separation challenge with Memphis musicians as the nexus. As the blanks fill, linking Rufus Thomas to Isaac Hayes to Alicia Keys to My Morning Jacket, for example, you realize that every note in the Memphis music story is a bridge to another sound, connected by inspiration.

Tour both museums on a $20 combination ticket, which includes a $5 voucher to use in either gift shop.

Memphis Music Hall of Fame, 126 Beale St., 901-205-2532,
memphismusichalloffame.com
Memphis Rock 'n' Soul Museum, 191 Beale St., #100, 901-205-2533,
memphisrocknsoul.org

FIND
SHANGRI-LA

Shangri-La Records

Buy or sell, new or used, vinyl or CD: Shangri-La Records entertains it all in that brown house on Madison Avenue, but you can bet the Memphis section (sections, rather) are loaded. So go on: Hunt for that rare Furry Lewis. Build your Big Star collection. Ransack the local bestsellers at the register for the *Beale Street Saturday Night* reissue. Don't be afraid to ask anyone behind the counter for guidance; in most cases, they're musicians themselves who'll do just about anything—even sell you the store copy of a release if it's the last in stock—to hook you up with Memphis music.

Bonus: During seasonal sales, many records go for $1
and bands perform on Shangri-La's porch or in the parking lot.
Target Purgefest in spring, Sweatfest in summer, and
the Purgeoning in fall. Concerts pop up at other times, too
(celebrating record releases and such), so be vigilant.

1916 Madison Ave.,
901-274-1916,
shangri.com

TOUR STAX
WITH A MEMPHIS HORN

Stax Museum of American Soul Music and Wayne Jackson Tours
The Stax Museum of American Soul Music is located on the site where Stax Records rocked before it was razed. Exhibits and recordings chronicle the studio's heart-tugging highs and lows, from black-and-white cooperation in an unlikely era to Otis Redding gone-too-soon and Stax's forced bankruptcy. Visit on your own or arrange a private tour of the museum with Wayne Jackson, sole surviving member of the Memphis Horns.

The film that intros the Stax experience gets me every time, but never so much as when I watched it with Jackson—he may tear up and brace you for support before taking your unanswered questions. Following the film, explore the museum alongside him, where episodes of *Soul Train* loop near a dance floor and Isaac Hayes's gold-plated Cadillac spins. In Studio A, Jackson details each musician's mark and the verve of the room in its heyday. (Tuesday afternoons in summer, live music once again fills the studio; check the museum's event calendar for performances by the Stax Music Academy Alumni Band and others.)

To extend your visit with Jackson, add on happy hour at his condo, decorated with 27 Gold Records and his Grammy Lifetime Achievement award.

Stax Museum of American Soul Music, 926 E. McLemore Ave., 901-942-7685, staxmuseum.com *Closed Monday*

Wayne Jackson Tours, 901-302-8911, waynejacksonmusic.com

SLIP
INTO SAM'S OFFICE

Sun Studio

When redevelopment of Memphis's Hotel Chisca began a few years back, Sun Studio employees hustled to save what they could of Dewey Phillips's DJ booth. They salvaged elements—acoustic tiles from the ceiling and walls, floors, control room glass—and reassembled them on the second floor of Sun Studio in 2014, 60 years after Phillips used the booth to introduce Elvis Presley to his radio audience.

After checking out Dewey's booth and the upstairs exhibits, you'll descend to the impossibly small studio that nurtured big dreams. The studio is, officially, where your tour ends. But Sun's staff has been hard at work again, this time retrofitting the control room to Sam Phillips's specs—going so far as to commission production of a single playback speaker based on Sam's design. After the crowd dissipates, ask your guide for a peek: It's a rare view from Sam's seat into the studio. Note that studio tours are available for visitors ages 5 and up.

> **Bonus:** Sun Studio's lobby is a sweet spot to order a milkshake, surrounded by all those records and photos of the Million Dollar Quartet, Howlin' Wolf, and Rufus Thomas, with a catchy soundtrack playing all the while.

706 Union Ave.,
800-441-6249,
sunstudio.com

LIVE
THE DREAM

Tad Pierson's American Dream Safari

Tad Pierson wants you to see, hear, smell, and rub elbows with Memphis. So he'll take you on a daytime drive of the city mapped by your interests; that's his Greatest Hits Tour. Just tell him what you're into and he'll chauffeur you around, windows down, for three hours, pointing out the stuff you want to see. I'd ask for a drive by Willie Mitchell's Royal Studios, where the late Mitchell's son, Boo, still produces music. But that's just me.

One more thing: Pierson will be picking you up in his hunk of a car, a 1955 Cadillac sized right for you and a few friends.

If it's Sunday morning, Pierson will take you to Al Green's Full Gospel Tabernacle, page 106. But if you want to experience Memphis's raw blues, let him take you on a Juke Joint Tour to neighborhood digs he keeps an ear to.

901-527-8870

BONUS:
3 MORE RIDES THAT ROCK

1. Backbeat Tours. Backbeat guides group bus and walking tours of all sorts, but the 90-minute Mojo Tour's the marquee with drive-bys of legendary-but-lost recording studios and the first Memphis homes of Johnny Cash, B.B. King. and Elvis Presley. P.S.: Your tour guide's a local musician who'll talk, and sing, you through the sights. Participation via onboard tambourines and shakers is voluntary. All Backbeat Tours, save the bar crawls, are suitable for any age. *143 Beale St., 901-272-2328, backbeattours.com*

2. Memphis Road Tours. Mike Freeman's been touring people around Memphis since 1998, while authoring guides on Elvis Presley and even living in Presley's first Memphis home. His private tours are as thorough as you'd expect them to be, stretching by request to Horn Lake, Mississippi, to Presley's Circle G Ranch. *901-289-7401, memphisroadtours.com*

3. Rockabilly Rides. What do Beale Street musicians do with free time and classic cars on their hands? If you're Brad Birkedahl and Brandon Cunning, you start a touring company. Solo or with a small group, hop in the '55 Bel Air or the '59 Skyliner for the Red, Hot & Blue Tour, a cruise through Elvis's early years in Memphis. *901-881-9192, rockabillyrides.com*

PACK IN FOR
A TINY BAR CONCERT

Bar DKDC

Karen Carrier's restaurants and bars, Mollie Fontaine Lounge, the Beauty Shop Restaurant + Lounge, and Bar DKDC serve up cocktails and sharing plates that know how to be whimsical *and* well done. Each concept occupies a space that takes "sense of place" to the edge. You should frequent them all. But since we're talking music, I need to make sure you get to Bar DKDC. Beyond food and drink, Carrier brings music to the space, regularly hosting too many local favorites to mention, though Motel Mirrors and Marcella & Her Lovers come through often. Pack in with the devotees, piling into the banquettes or standing as needed.

964 S. Cooper St.,
901-272-0830,
bardkdc.com
Closed Sunday and Monday

COME HOME,
MUSIC LOVER

B.B. King's Blues Club, starring Memphis Jones

You might know a lot about Memphis music. Memphis Jones knows more. And so his show goes at B.B. King's Beale Street Blues Club—a music history lesson set to . . . well, you know. As Jones's narrative weaves through backstories and feels down the fringes of the city's musical patchwork, you're reminded that the threads of popular music unraveled from Beale Street. Jones's set list, ranging from the Box Tops' "The Letter" to Mahalia Jackson's "Move on up a Little Higher," won't let you forget it.

> **Bonus:** Jones pulls the early shift at B.B. King's
> (5–7:30 p.m., Monday evenings) and keeps the volume low,
> presenting the perfect Memphis music primer for junior rockers.

143 Beale St.,
901-524-5464,
bbkingclubs.com

BONUS:
5 MORE THINGS TO DO ON BEALE STREET AT NIGHT

1. Soak up the vibe. Half the allure is the street itself, so before committing to any bar or club, just walk. I like to start around 7 p.m. at the west end of Beale and progress east. En route, order a go-cup from any walk-up bar and watch the Beale Street Flippers turn the cobblestone street into a runway for aerial somersaults.

2. Hail the Queen. Discuss the night's agenda over drinks in Silky O'Sullivan's open-air courtyard. Before 8 p.m., the crowd is a hodgepodge of parents inching their toddlers near Silky's resident goats and friends sharing the bar's signature "Diver," a gallon-sized cocktail served in a bucket. They're all accessories to Barbara Blue, who commands the bar with her powerhouse vocals during sets Wednesday through Sunday. *183 Beale St., 901-522-9596, silkyosullivans.com*

3. Dance with the locals. Outside of winter, locals gather 'round the W.C. Handy statue in his namesake park for free concerts that stretch from late afternoon to late evening (Fridays and Saturdays). The experience is electric no matter who's playing; no matter if you're people-watching or throwing yourself into the mix. *200 Beale St.*

4. Make yourself at home. A nominal cover gets you into Blues Hall. Inside the narrow room, strands of white lights drape along the ceiling and framed paintings hang on the walls, giving it the feel of someone's living room. The bands that play here strip down their soul and blues sounds for intimate sets, a cozy warm-up to what comes next.

5. Groove on out. Blues Hall is connected to Rum Boogie Café, so you get two experiences for one cover charge. Walk through the adjoining door for a sight- and soundscape that's altogether different: Inside Rum Boogie, neon lights spelling STAX glow red, and at least once a week around 9 p.m., Vince Johnson and the Boogie Blues Band take the stage—harmonica, sax, Hammond organ, and all—so when they groove out to "Green Onions" or "Walking the Dog," it sounds to me like Beale Street live music should. *Blues Hall/Rum Boogie Café, 182 Beale St., 901-528-0150, rumboogie.com*

Note: Any night on Beale Street can be family-friendly, but Fridays and Saturdays at 9 p.m., a security checkpoint goes up, ensuring that guests coming onto the street are 21 or older. Minors already on the street at this time are permitted to stay, accompanied by a parent, until 11 p.m. After 11 p.m. on Fridays and Saturdays, Beale goes 21 and up.

CENTER YOURSELF

Center for Southern Folklore

If you haven't been to the Center for Southern Folklore, I'll forgive you. But you darn sure better get there before I ask you again.

The Center leads something of a double life: Its vivid, sound-soaked party space fronts an ambitious mission to preserve Delta culture. Center co-founder Judy Peiser's been at it since 1972, gathering audio, films, and photographs of Southern crafters, farmers, and musicians.

Back to the party: At an age most would fade into retirement, Peiser's still staying up late, passing around a tip jar for the acts she books most Friday and Saturday nights. Her bookings give credence to every musical expression from throwback sounds to contemporary currents, though friends of the Center make repeat and memorable appearances, Daddy Mack Blues Band and Zeke Johnson among them. The common thread: Peiser puts artists on stage who tell a story through their music.

So go. Pay the nominal cover charge. Order a beer or greens and cornbread or cobbler. Put something in the tip jar for the performers, and buy one of their CDs, or a little chunk of folk art, a vintage concert bill, or a photo from the Center's archive. The Center's put me onto some of my favorite bands to follow around town. I promise it'll do the same for you.

123 S. Main St.,
901-525-3655,
southernfolklore.com

HAUNT
EARNESTINE & HAZEL'S

Earnestine & Hazel's

It's an ex-brothel! It's haunted! The Rolling Stones wrote songs about it! *Esquire* said you should go! Get to Earnestine & Hazel's and tell me why *you* treasure the place. Is it the jukebox that rocks seamlessly from Booker T. & the MGs to Talking Heads? The peeling paint and soft-spotted stairs that signal this building's been around? The upstairs rooms scattered with cast-off furniture and ancient electronics? The open windows that frame that frozen-in-time feel of South Main Street? The soul burger, page 87? These are my reasons. What are yours?

> **Tip:** Arrive early for a solitary experience, particularly if you want to appreciate the singularity of the upstairs. To feel the energy of the crowd, show late, say, 11 p.m. on a Friday or Saturday.

531 S. Main St.,
901-523-9754,
earnestineandhazelsjukejoint.com

RETURN
TO LAFAYETTE'S

Lafayette's Music Room

Talk to Memphians of a certain age and they'll tell you about catching Billy Joel and other big names as unknowns. The venue was Lafayette's Music Room in Overton Square, page 44. By the mid-1980s, however, Memphis's collective party had migrated to a different part of town. Both the venue and much of the district went dark.

In 2012, the scene began to change. Just before Christmas, local artists debuted pop-up shops in Overton Square's vacant buildings. Neighbors gathered for a tree-lighting on the Square's defining corner (North Cooper Street and Madison Avenue). By New Year's Day 2013, the Square was on its way back, with plans to resurrect Lafayette's along with it.

Today, Lafayette's is back to hosting nightly concerts—daily ones too, on weekends—by local, regional, and national touring musicians. The wrought-iron second-story balcony will charm you, but head inside for the intimate performances Lafayette's is legendary for. Weekend brunch is perfect for chilling out to Memphis sounds—bluesy Susan Marshall, funky instrumentals by Joe Restivo—and these lower-volume shows are particularly family-friendly. Return after dark for a different sound every night, from total rock-outs to acoustic sets. Lucky you if it's John Paul Keith with a friend like Dave Cousar sitting in.

2119 Madison Ave.,
901-207-5097,
lafayettes.com/memphis

● ●

GET A SHELL
OF A DEAL

Levitt Shell

What does a night of live music cost? Tickets plus service fees plus merch, if you have any money left? Not at the Levitt Shell. Thanks to a partnership with the Levitt Foundation (mission: building communities by providing free live music), Memphis's Shell gifts you 50 free concerts a year. So pack coolers/picnic baskets and blankets/chairs. Bring cash for the donation buckets or stations, and if you don't have time for a beer run, buy it on-site to benefit the Shell; food trucks usually pull up, too. As you're sitting under the stars, bewitched by the sound, consider:

• Memphis's Shell was built with help from the WPA in 1936. Twenty-seven WPA-connected band shells were built nationwide around that time, but Memphis's Shell is one of the last standing.

• A few weeks after Dewey Phillips, page 117, introduced Elvis Presley to his radio audience in July 1954, Elvis opened on this stage for Slim Whitman. No biggie . . . just the widely acknowledged first-ever rock-and-roll show.

The Levitt Shell is located inside Overton Park,
which is bounded by North Parkway, East Parkway,
Poplar Avenue, and McLean Boulevard;
levittshell.org

BONUS:
5 MORE PLACES TO LISTEN UP

1. Buccaneer Lounge. Small, dark, and smoky for those nights you want to cozy up to a bar and live music. *1368 Monroe Ave., 901-278-0909, facebook.com/BuccaneerLounge*

2. The Cove. People call this a dive, but The Cove isn't playing around with its food or cocktail menu, and the vibe is more nautical-swank than crusty bar. Live music Thursday through Saturday night. *2559 Broad Ave., 901-730-0719, thecovememphis.com*

3. The Hi-Tone Café. Near-nightly bookings shuffle variety through town, but there's always room on the Hi-Tone stage for homegrown bands. *412–414 N. Cleveland St., 901-490-0335, hitonememphis.com*

4. Otherlands Coffee Bar. This homey coffee den hosts all-ages, smoke-free shows Friday and Saturday nights. Join the Otherlands Live Facebook group for details. *641 S. Cooper St., 901-278-4994, otherlandscoffeebar.com*

5. St. John's United Methodist Church. You might not equate church with Friday night, concerts, or a recording artist/reverend like Dr. John Kilzer. Yet these elements merge during a 6 p.m. service of recovery called The Way, where everyone's welcome to share in Kilzer's healing message and music. The changing line-up of supporting musicians could include Kirk Whalum or Jim Spake and Rick Steff of my favorite Memphis band, Lucero. *1207 Peabody Ave., 901-726-4104, stjohnsmidtown.org/worship/the-way*

CIRCUIT
THESE FESTIVALS

Essential music festivals

Beale Street Music Festival. BSMF sounds off on four stages in downtown's Tom Lee Park, making it possible for you to hear, say, Paul Simon and Memphis rapper Yo Gotti on the same ticket. *memphisinmay.org/musicfestival; late April/early May*

Gonerfest. As a label, Goner Records embodies an eclectic sound with live energy. Gonerfest puts 40 relevant global acts on Midtown Memphis stages, including some free shows near the Goner Records store. *goner-records.com/gonerfest; September*

International Blues Challenge. The world's largest assemblage of blues musicians gathers on Beale Street for this battle of the bands. Target Tuesday or Wednesday night of the Challenge to get an earful without battling crowds. *blues.org; January*

Memphis Music & Heritage Festival. A true genre-bender where you're as likely to hear gospel as garage rock. Unfolds inside the Center for Southern Folklore, page 124, and along the South Main Street mall. *southernfolklore.com; September*

Rock for Love. This benefit for Memphis's Church Health Center, celebrating its 10th year in 2016, doubles as an orientation to some of the city's most accessible acts in some of its most accessible (Midtown Memphis) venues. *rockforlove.org; September*

STALK
THIS BAND

Sons of Mudboy

Mudboy and the Neutrons, though active for decades and heavily influential, was a tough act to pin down live. And by summer 2013, founding members Lee Baker, Jim Dickinson, and Sid Selvidge had passed away. But their sons, Ben Baker, Cody and Luther Dickinson, and Steve Selvidge, along with surviving "Mudboy" Jimmy Crosthwait and supporting musicians, come together on rare occasions as Sons of Mudboy. The challenge is chasing the occasions. Wait for the brothers Dickinson to come in off the road with North Mississippi Allstars, and for Selvidge to break from touring with the Hold Steady. Follow the group's stirrings on Facebook. Watch event listings for Bar DKDC, page 120, and Minglewood Hall, where the band's been known to turn up. Then come out and listen to the legacy.

facebook.com/SonsOfMudboy

BONUS:
5 MORE SUPER-GROUPS TO CATCH WHILE YOU'RE IN TOWN

1. The Bo-Keys. If these funky grooves sound familiar, it's because you're hearing musicians who've backed Stax and Hi Records superstars, among others. *thebokeys.com*

2. Bluff City Backsliders. Banjos, fiddles, and mandolins whipped into a barrelhouse frenzy. *facebook.com/bluffcitybacksliders*

3. Devil Train. A bluegrass attack featuring banjo virtuoso Randall Morton. *facebook.com/DevilTrain*

4. Hope Clayburn's Soul Scrimmage. The only woman I know who can play two saxophones at once, backed by a band that'll make you want to dance. *facebook.com/hopeclayburnmusic*

5. Mighty Souls Brass Band. A party of brass that's known to march right off the stage and into the crowd. *mightysoulsbrassband.com*

ADDITIONAL TOURS
AND RESOURCES

First, the resources:

choose901.com
A clearinghouse for news from every angle of Memphis life.
Watch for "The Weekender" posts to program your free time.

memphistravel.com
Digital features to inspire your exploration, free downloads of the
annual visitor guide and city app, interactive maps . . . plus daily
updates on where to eat and what to do, including "5 Things to Do
This Weekend" posts, at **ilovememphisblog.com**.

4 MORE WAYS
TO GET AROUND TOWN

General sightseeing and transportation options

1. Carriage Company of Memphis. Downtown, hail a horse-drawn carriage outside The Peabody, page 12, or where Beale Street meets South Second and South Third Streets. You can also call for pickup almost anywhere downtown. Choose a 30-, 45-, or 60-minute ride to take in the surrounds. *901-507-2587, carriagecomemphis.com*

2. Downtown Trolleys. While Memphis's fleet of vintage trolleys is in flux, you can ride rubber-wheel facsimiles along the standard routes: Main Street, connecting districts from The Pinch to South Main; Riverfront, a loop that compounds the Main Street line with a stretch along the Mississippi River; and Madison, serving the medical district on the eastern edge of downtown. Look for stations throughout downtown and Midtown, and bring exact change for the fare box: Base fare is $1 one way; an all-day pass is available from your driver for $3.50. *matatransit.com/services/trolleys; no Madison Line service on Sunday*

3. Memphis Hop. This shuttle loops major attractions citywide. Choose the line that suits your plans; then hop on and off as you wish. Hop tickets are valid for 24 hours, and children ages 5 and under ride free. Note that attraction admission is not included, and shuttle frequency lessens November through March. *901-577-5467, memphishop.com*

4. Ride the Roo. See that kangaroo cheesing with a martini? That's the Roo, a shuttle bus that hops between a dozen Overton Square and Cooper-Young stops Friday and Saturday nights, 5 p.m.–2 a.m. Buy a $2 ride or an all-night pass for $5. *ridetheroo.com*

GIVE BACK

St. Jude Children's Research Hospital Tour

For all that Memphis gives you, here's one way to give back:

It's hard to imagine that St. Jude Children's Research Hospital, today with 3,600 employees in Memphis, boosted by outreach efforts in 17 countries, began as a deal founder Danny Thomas struck with the patron saint of lost causes. A free, hour-long tour conveys the organization's history and mission: to treat children with incurable diseases no matter their background or ability to pay. In the Patient Care Center, you'll pass parents pulling patients in red wagons; in the Research Building, you'll learn of St. Jude's total therapy approach (that's also where you'll rub the nose of a sculpted Danny Thomas for good luck). All tours must be scheduled in advance, which is an ideal time to ask:

- Will the Pavilion be open during your visit? That's the gold-domed building on campus that highlights Danny Thomas as an entertainer and humanitarian alongside St. Jude milestones. Special events close it from time to time (call 901-595-4414 to find out), but you can always step into the adjacent memorial garden, where Danny and wife, Rose Marie, are buried. Note that hospital tours are available for visitors ages 16 and up; the Pavilion is open to all ages.

- Want to donate blood or platelets while you're on-site? Call ahead to the Blood Donor Center (901-595-2024) for a short pre-screen and to schedule an appointment before or after your tour.

332 N. Lauderdale St.,
901-578-2042,
stjude.org

SUGGESTED
ITINERARIES

The following itineraries aren't intended to be exhaustive, but they will jumpstart your exploration of some of Memphis's quintessential neighborhoods. Remember that local tour guides and transport services can help you get around. See pages 118-119 and 134 for ideas.

DOWNTOWN

If you read this far, you know what to do in the Beale Street Historic District, pages 4 and 121-123, South Main Historic Arts District, page 46, and along the Mississippi Riverfront, pages 10 and 65. For something different, walk downtown's Edge District, where you can tour Sun Studio, page 117, and St. Blues Guitar Workshop, page 112, grab a bite at Trolley Stop Market, page 85, and sample craft beer at High Cotton Brewing Co., page 95.

MIDTOWN

I've already detailed the Broad Avenue Arts District, page 30, and Crosstown, page 35, so let's focus on Cooper-Young and Overton Square, your ready-made night(s) out. In Cooper-Young, enjoy craft beer at Memphis Made Brewing Co., page 95, dinner at Tsunami, page 88, and live music at Bar DKDC, page 120. In Overton Square, nab a patio table for dinner and drinks at The Second Line, page 91, then see who's playing at Lafayette's Music Room, page 126. With reservations, do dinner at Bari, page 88, and a show at any of the Square's theaters, page 44.

EAST

Select your speed: a measured stroll through the Dixon Gallery & Gardens, page 38, or an all-out romp (with kids) through My Big Backyard at Memphis Botanic Garden, page 66. Do lunch at Porcellino's Craft Butcher, page 91, or the East Memphis outpost of LYFE Kitchen, page 99, followed by dessert at the original Muddy's Bake Shop (5101 Sanderlin Ave., #114; closed Sunday). A walk through the Crystal Shrine Grotto at Memorial Park Cemetery, page 20, isn't far.

STAX AREA

I prefer visiting the Stax Museum of American Soul Music, page 116, in the afternoon, partly because that's when the museum hosts free concerts (Tuesdays from summer into fall) and partly because it leaves the morning for meandering nearby Elmwood Cemetery/working up an appetite for lunch at The Four Way, page 82. Read more about Elmwood on page 19.

GRACELAND AREA

Do this on a Sunday: Start early to take advantage of free walk-ups to Graceland's Meditation Garden and uncrowded photo ops at the mansion's gates, page 110 (check Graceland's website before you go to confirm that walk-ups are permitted the day of your visit). If you choose to tour the mansion, you'll have a couple of hours before service begins at Al Green's Full Gospel Tabernacle, page 106. When church dismisses, beeline it to Uncle Lou's Fried Chicken, page 84, for a sweet, spicy treat.

WITH KIDS

I'll find a way to make just about anything in town kid-friendly, which explains why my daughter loves Amy LaVere so, and can brief you on High Cotton Brewing Co.'s hops. Still, my daughter and her visiting cousins beg for certain Memphis kid-essentials, including:

- **Playing downtown.** Go for breakfast or lunch at The Arcade, page 79. Catch the duck march at The Peabody Memphis, page 12. Wage family trivia contests at the Cotton Museum, page 11. Gawk at the indoor cypress swamp at Bass Pro Shops at the Pyramid, page 10. Run through the splash pad at Beale Street Landing, page 10. Order ice cream at A. Schwab's soda fountain, page 4. (With train enthusiasts, pop into the Memphis Railroad & Trolley Museum, page 13.)

- **Hanging in the center of the city.** Smack in the middle of Memphis, in one tidy triangle, I can plot points to please every kid in my life: Tobey Skate Park, page 73, for my nephew Max. The Children's Museum of Memphis, page 60, for my nephew Jameson. The Pink Palace Museum, page 22, for my niece Kalista. Benjamin L. Hooks Central Library, page 52, for my daughter. And slices for all from Rock'n Dough Pizza Co., page 79.

- **Doing it themselves.** Watch for free family days with art-making activities at the Memphis Brooks Museum of Art, page 34, and the Dixon Gallery & Gardens, page 38. Then, check the calendars of these maker spaces: The Art Project, Bumbletees Sewing Studio, and Sew Memphis, page 32, and CLOUD901, page 52.

- **Not sitting still.** pages 57-73 (don't miss the Rec Room, page 74).

- **Devouring other kid-approved eats** at Lunchbox Eats, page 82, Trolley Stop Market, page 85, Huey's, page 87, and Shelby Forest General Store, page 86. For dessert, hit Jerry's Sno Cones, page 92, or La Michoacana, page 89.

- **Rocking out.** To treat the whole family to live Memphis music, try Memphis Jones's show at B.B. King's Blues Club, page 121, weekend brunch at Lafayette's Music Room, page 126, or any show at the Levitt Shell, page 127.

FREE
ACTIVITIES

ACTIVITIES
BY SEASON

A few suggestions to get you started . . .

WINTER

International Blues Challenge, 129

Martin Luther King Jr. Day at the National Civil Rights Museum, 14

Old Forest bird-watching, 67

SPRING

Beale Street Music Festival, 129

Broad Avenue Art Walk, 30

Farmers market season opens, 101

Ghost River Outfitters paddling trips, 62

Jimmy Ogle Bridge Walks, 9

Memphis Redbirds baseball, 69

Memphis Riverboats, 7

Midtown Opera Festival, 42

Shelby Forest General Store porch music series, 86

Urban Barn Market, 49

Wiseacre Brewing Co. Taste the Rarity Beer Festival, 95

World Championship Barbecue Cooking Contest, 81

SUMMER

FALL

INDEX